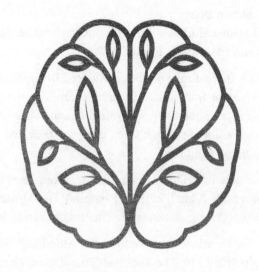

ENCOUNTER

SHAWN BOLZ

CHARISMA
HOUSE

Most Charisma Media products are available at special quantity discounts for bulk purchase for sales promotions, premiums, fundraising, and educational needs. For details, call us at (407) 333-0600 or visit our website at www.charismamedia.com.

Encounter by Shawn Bolz
Published by Charisma House, an imprint of Charisma Media
600 Rinehart Road, Lake Mary, Florida 32746

Copyright © 2022 by Shawn Bolz
All rights reserved

Visit the author's website at bolzministries.com.

Cataloging-in-Publication Data is on file with the Library of Congress.
International Standard Book Number: 978-1-63641-055-5
E-book ISBN: 978-1-63641-056-2

22 23 24 25 26 — 9 8 7 6 5 4 3 2 1
Printed in the United States of America.

I want to dedicate this book to my wife, Cherie Bolz, who sees me with God's eyes and is constantly telling me what that looks like, which in turn gives me faith and courage to communicate things like this.
I also want to love on my daughters, Harper and Hartley, and thank them for loving me so well. I love you infinity, infinity, infinity eleven! Lock your hearts; I'll never let you go!

CONTENTS

ACKNOWLEDGMENTS

I WANT TO THANK Stephen Strang and the Charisma Media team for challenging me to put this book out there and then walking with me through the process.

The kinds of encounters I share in this book were historically hidden for niche groups of people, oftentimes too risky to share. I love that Charisma is bold enough to chronicle encounters that can help shape Christianity and help us partner with Jesus to receive vision, without which we might just perish.

Charisma's partnership in releasing my articles, podcasts, and content on the Charisma Podcast Network, on Charisma News, and in *Charisma* magazine has been instrumental in shaping my life, journey, and ministry voice. Thank you, Charisma team, for your friendship, your belief, and your faith.

I also want to thank my team at Bolz Ministries, especially Jeremy Butrous, who was the one who told me I should write this book and that the world needs to hear my encounters. Your ability to believe in others and lead with God's heart has inspired me so many times, and Jeremy, you just might be right about this book.

I want to thank Bob Hasson and his wife, Lauren, who have

walked with me. These encounters and the spiritual perspective I have are birthing conversations in the marketplace through our podcast and other projects we have been doing together. You have been an instrument in God's hands and one of the rarest gifts in our lives. Thank you, friends.

I also want to thank my TBN family, namely Matthew and Laurie Crouch, for constantly putting our content in front of the world and believing that an encounter with God is worth everything.

And finally, thank you, team (people too numerous to name), for encouraging me.

FOREWORD

WE ARE LIVING in unprecedented times. In John 21 the disciples were fishing all night and caught nothing, but Jesus told them to cast their nets one more time on the right side of the boat. The result was a huge catch of fish. I believe we are on the verge of a John 21 moment. Prophetically speaking, this large catch represents the great revival that the Lord wants to bring as we approach the end of the age.

Several years ago I had an encounter with the Lord in which He showed me some things about this great move of God. First, He told me, "Do not settle for a form of godliness that lacks power." This word was significant for me because I spent most of my formative years as a young believer studying Scripture and theology in college and seminary. Second, He revealed that this coming revival would be rooted in His Word and encounters with the living God, accompanied by supernatural manifestations of His goodness and glory.

In chapter 6 of this book, Shawn talks about the attack on the Josephs—the dreamers who cast God's vision for the future. I have lived through a Joseph season in which I had to endure betrayal and the pit. But God in His goodness gave me a super-natural encounter beforehand. He told me that He would use all the pain of that season to prepare me for His greater purpose. Encounters with God at crucial moments have changed the course of my life and given me the faith to move forward against all odds and obstacles.

Encounters have not just personally shaped my life and ministry of Fusion Global but have shaped history. The Bible is a divine record and testimony of the world-changing power of God encounters. The Lord never intended for supernatural encounters to be limited to biblical times. God wants to give each one of us personal encounters with Him. The Lord also wants us to learn from other people's encounters. This need to learn is why what Shawn shares in this book is so critical for the time in which we live. There is so much wisdom and revelation we can glean from these encounters that Shawn shares—I believe they will change many lives! There is also such a strong anointing on this book that I could feel a new fire being lit in my heart to seek fresh encounters as I read it.

God encounters build faith and shed light on biblical truth. Today more than ever, we need to hear God's voice and learn from people like Shawn, who has uniquely encountered God. There are few spiritual leaders like Shawn Bolz. Not only is his prophetic gifting off the charts, but he embodies the love of God and has a huge heart for justice.

Shawn's ability to communicate both prophetic experiences and wisdom in a very accessible, nonreligious, and practical way sets him—and this book—apart. However, what I believe makes this book special are the keys to activating supernatural encounters in one's life and Shawn's critical insights into how to process these encounters. *Encounter* is an important work that we desperately need at this time and season. I know all who read it will be significantly blessed, as I was.

Rabbi Jason Sobel is the founder of Fusion Global, a ministry that seeks to bring people into the full inheritance of the faith by connecting treasures of the old and the new. He received his rabbinic ordination from the Union of Messianic Jewish Congregations in 2005 and has a Bachelor of Arts in Jewish studies and a Master of Arts in intercultural studies. He is the author of several books, including the best-selling Mysteries of the Messiah: Unveiling Divine Connections From Genesis to Today. *He is also the coauthor with Kathie Lee Gifford of the* New York Times *best seller* The Rock, the Road, and the Rabbi *and is the spiritual adviser to* The Chosen *TV series and host of* The Chosen Unveiled *on TBN.*

INTRODUCTION

A LL MY REVELATIONS and visions have led me to the point of releasing this book to you.

Some people have read some of my other books, been part of our events, heard my podcasts, watched me on TV, or even been part of our mentoring platform online yet haven't heard some of the rich encounters that have defined my theology and love-based, hope-fueled perspective. Yet so much of what I have built a platform to share has come out of several core encounters I had with God, which have truly given me understanding into things I never would have known. They have given me a spiritual perspective and supernatural awareness that inspire the gifts and voice I have today.

I am writing this book to share those encounters because I believe you too can be released and commissioned into new ways of thinking. You might also experience an expansion of your spiritual intelligence as you see through my spiritual eyes things that point to Jesus, review our role on this earth, and even highlight the urgency of His return.

When I wrote *Keys to Heaven's Economy* in 2005, I wrote about a series of visitations. I didn't define a lot of what I saw; I let the visitations speak for themselves. The book became a phenomenon, and people all over the world have shared how they were impacted by these sometimes allegorical visions.

I never thought I would write something like it again, but because I met with God in a unique way, I experienced a series of encounters over a decade that tied together so well I felt I had to share them. I am hoping they inspire you as well.

I also share stories of things that happened to me that were due to God's prophetic leading. When you have an encounter like this, God often has you walk something out to give you more insight into it, and He has you become the encounter for other believers you share it with. Just as the Old Testament prophets often walked out prophetic journeys that were symbolic for Israel, prophetic people nowadays can walk something out that becomes a message for the church.

My prayer is that this book gives you a new or fresh vision of your Christianity, helping you walk out your faith exactly as God intended and in a way you have hungered for. I also pray it helps you see some things God has been preparing you to see all along.

If you are like me and have a hard time with parabolic, allegorical, or visionary language, I encourage you to give this book a try and see if there is inspiration to be found. So much of what is in here is not literal but spiritual, so it can be interpreted many different ways. But my heart and goal are that the teaching in these pages would only enhance your experience with the Bible and prayer.

I share a lot of my own life experiences and parallel them to spiritual themes God was showing me at different times. I know this can sometimes be mistaken for self-indulgence or self-importance, but I have no intention of drawing focus to me. I write this only to share from my life and heart for your benefit—so you can see what I see.

In these pages is an encounter-based view of concepts most

evangelical theologians believe are true. What I share is experiential; however, I believe the encounters will help you better relate to what the Bible teaches. The insights I have gleaned from these encounters are not anti-biblical but would be considered extra biblical. However, I stay true to the basic tenets of the faith outlined in the Bible, not straying from or adding to that truth but trying to give you my experience of it.

Some of the encounters and visions I've had have led me to study fields that were never on my radar and to search for language to best express how our great and beautiful God wired us to walk out our connection to and with Him. This caused me to care about neurology, neurobiology, psychology, and the environment. I believe encounters with God should lead us to care about what God is doing all over the world in various fields, not just the ones we had passion for before the encounters.

The children of Israel were given practical strategies for how to thrive and build and cultivate their culture, nation, and land. Similarly, God is giving the body of Christ revelations that are church centered but that will also bless the world. The revelations He is releasing are about how to thrive in the entire world, not just in ministry.

We are the most unique beings in the universe other than God because not only are we made in His image; we are an imprint of God's very nature. We have the capacity to manifest God's glory through our partnership with Jesus in a way that will set the whole earth back to God's original plan and order by the end of the age. If we could understand our spiritual, neurological, psychological, and even physical connection to God, we could bring His changes to every problem humanity faces. A lot of these solutions may originate through our incredible, supernatural connection to God, but they will come in the form of practical wisdom and even scientific solutions.

The closer we get to the return of Christ, the more distorted mainstream issues such as those found in psychology, science, politics, education, and media become. That is what we are seeing now on a grand scale. But God will be releasing Christians to demonstrate what His love looks like in these same areas. It does not matter how dark it gets; that just sets the stage for the illumination of all that God is and for His glory to shine more profoundly through people like you and me.

We are about to come into a great time of light. These perplexing issues of our time will be disrupted, in a heavenly way, by believers who not only express the principles of their faith but also release tangible resources for people to experience it. We see this in the Bible—for every Egyptian and Babylonian experience there was a Daniel, Esther, or Joseph to deliver God's will and protect His people. Many times they brought blessing or balance to a worldly, secular culture as well.

You are going to find that the encounters in this book inspired action on my part, and they shaped much of the last eighteen years of my life. Hopefully faith will come by your "hearing" these encounters because God is making so much available to you in so many ways! My prayer is that this encounter will become your encounter and you will find yourself in these pages as you read them.

CHAPTER 1

THE BEGINNING OF
THE ENCOUNTER

I WAS POSITIONED ON a ridge overlooking a valley. Although I knew this was a vision, the experience was so real to my senses. I was looking over an area in the valley that was being developed by an ancient civilization. It was not like watching a TV channel because all my senses were active as if I were there. I could smell the thick desert air, and my eyes were partially blinded by the hot afternoon sun, yet it was still a vision. I could see people of all types down below, and they were building things. There was so much construction going on that I did not know where to look first, and because of my lack of education on ancient architecture, I couldn't completely understand what was being done in the various areas.

There were so many different laborers around. It was astounding just how many thousands of people were working. I saw roads being paved with historical materials. I zoomed in to what seemed to be a planning area, with men pointing at architectural maps or systems. Buildings were being designated for certain places. It was all being so well planned it was almost mythical.

I was watching a masterful city being re-created from the

ground up, but I didn't know exactly what I was looking at until I saw the tens of thousands of laborers in the middle of it all. One of the future wonders of all mankind—a building people had been waiting to be built since the fall of man—was becoming a reality. Up until this point, I thought I was seeing a parabolic vision, a parable of sorts that was one of the most powerful demonstrations of God's imagination in my own. But now I knew God was showing me one of humanity's greatest events: the construction of the temple in ancient Israel.

∽

The Israelites were busy working, but foreigners living in Israel had also been conscripted to help build. Can you imagine seventy thousand men just carrying materials, eighty thousand men cutting stone in the hills, and thirty-six hundred foremen overseeing them? What did other kingdoms think about this structure that was unlike anything anyone had ever seen or imagined, or the fact that everyone was busily working to build a temple to the God who was known to love His people, not just indenture them into servitude?

As the foundation was being laid for the temple of God, I could hear the loud sounds of stones moving and construction happening, and I could see animals maneuvering around the construction through bustling, primitive but beautiful streets. There was also a strange hush in the midst of the noise, as if everyone knew they were working on something that had never been created before. I compare it to modern construction workers working on a building in a large city such as New York, without the carnal and sometimes lowbrow working environment that you picture in modern construction sites. The atmosphere was solemn, but it wasn't like the quiet you find in a library. There was a general joy and anticipation in the air, as if this generation of Israelites knew God had chosen them to build this structure, that they were part of something that would so mark history that people would remember what was happening before and after this moment in time.

I was given a bird's-eye view of the whole region and found myself swooping over streets, housing, marketplaces, walls, and finally, again, to the construction underway at the temple site. I could see into a magnificent staging area, where a group of men was looking over plans and designs, and in the middle was a man right out of the Bible. I knew him immediately, not because of my biblical knowledge about the temple being built, though I am sure that was somewhere within me, but because he was absolutely unlike anyone else the world has ever seen. He had the joyful countenance of a man groomed for God's greatness. His ruddy good looks, his dark skin, the depth of wisdom in his eyes, and the life experience only David's son could have carried made it clear to me—this was Solomon.

I knew I was looking at Solomon early in his reign—before the coming splendor God would regale him with—yet he was majestic. Being the son of King David had created a culture, or air, about him that made him stunning to observe. How he carried himself and coordinated with those around him was a sight to behold. He carried a presence that came from within him and radiated to all those who were serving him. I felt what people must feel when they are around top Olympic athletes on gold medal day or Wall Street brokers radiating the glory of watching the stock market make its largest closing in history. I was beholding this man in all his glory. He was awe-inspiring, yet it was not just his characteristics that defined him. Even more than his being a glorious man, I could see and sense potential inside him that drew heaven's attention.

I looked at a realm beyond the natural things I was seeing, and there, beyond the veil of humanity, I saw the spiritual reality. I saw that not only was Solomon surrounded by expert builders and influential men; he also had an audience of the angelic. Heaven seemed to be buzzing as much as the construction I was watching. Heavenly beings that were indescribable were flying in all directions, and the whole area seemed to be encircled by an army in the sky that was so vast I couldn't imagine trying to count all its members.

Up to this point, I had only been watching this vision, but now a spiritual being standing next to Solomon looked up at the small spot I was canvasing the area from. He seemed to see me. It scared me at first, as it might if you were watching an epic movie and suddenly one of the characters looked right at you. Not only did the being see me; he came and stood next to me. He was in a realm that was just beyond my normal sight, so he appeared blurry—like an even blurrier Monet painting hanging between me and the objects in the vision. He moved like liquid, and I was both afraid and intrigued when I saw him. I knew this heavenly being was an angel, but I wouldn't understand the depth of what I was seeing until later.

A voice rang out that sounded like it was on amplified speakers: "This is an important time in Solomon's day." There was comfort in what he said, and I acted as if I knew what he was talking about, but I didn't know at all. We watched for what seemed to be a year. The atmosphere was so pregnant with his words. I was imagining why it was so important, but I was too afraid to talk.

Then my vision of the construction started to speed up, as if it were being fast-forwarded, and what took years in human time happened in my vision in several minutes. I watched glorious structures such as schools, great marketplaces, and housing all being built in one sudden moment, and I watched agricultural development at the same time in the distance.

In the heavens above the construction, in this fast-forward part of my vision, things seemed just as active. It reminded me of a busy airport, with many planes coming and going, but instead of watching a coordinated effort of planes, it seemed as if angels were everywhere, visiting and depositing part of God's very nature throughout the region. It was almost as if I were watching spiritual agriculture—God's nature being planted like seeds in the people below. Something was getting sown that had never been sown before.

But what I was focused on was what everyone in the city was interested in: the temple. Being an American in this century, I did not have the awareness of what this temple meant to the children of Israel, who had been carrying an ark around to defeat enemies and intimidate their oppressors. I did not understand what Solomon was departing from to create this God-commissioned structure when all he had known to date was to worship in the tabernacle of David. I did not understand the holiness of the room called the holy of holies. But I knew it was all breathtaking even before I had any education about it.

The people all around were on a crash course, being prepared for something that had not been present in humanity since the Garden of Eden. God's presence was going to cohabitate with them. They were going to experience the benefit of this not only in their worship but also in their families, in their education, in their judicial system, in their city infrastructure, in their agriculture, and in their politics. Everything was being prepared to bring about a city and people that thrived under the presence of God.

SOLOMON'S CRY

Then the angelic man pointed, and I was brought into an almost face-to-face vision of Solomon. Things were happening inside of him too. He was being prepared for the presence of God, and I could sense in him a cry that was, surprisingly, not romantic or poetic like his father's; it was a cry birthed out of deep frustration. He knew he could not do things the same way his father, David, had, and he needed more.

King David himself said he had not been chosen to build the temple because of the blood on his hands (1 Chron. 28:2–3). David had a golden heart, but he sometimes used barbarian methods to rule. Solomon was pregnant with a new vision for his kingship. He saw the potential of having the presence of God on His people. Solomon was tasked from heaven with building the greatest structure humanity had ever known, and he was to use the greatest resources on the known earth to build it, but he had to do it with peace, through relationship, not through battles and war claims over resources.

Solomon began to negotiate inside and outside of his kingdom for the resources he needed. He knew how to distribute the wealth that had been stored up for the mission at hand. Even before his epic encounter with God, when the Lord asked him what he wanted, Solomon was born to rule with wisdom. He had an uncanny sense of the right way to build that affected every quadrant of society. He wasn't just building a temple and a palace; *he was kingdom shaping.*

Then we have the biblical passage of God appearing to Solomon—a man with riches and a desire to honor God—and saying, "Ask what I might give to you" (2 Chron. 1:7, MEV).

Solomon answered, "Give me the ability to have Your mind, Your perceptions, and Your wisdom as if You were ruling Your people through me, for who is able to govern this great people of Yours?" (See 2 Chronicles 1:10.)

Now this was a key moment in time. God was excited, and it showed.

> Then God responded to Solomon, "Because this was in your heart and you did not ask for possessions, wealth, and honor, or even the life of those who hate you, nor have you asked for many days of life, but you have asked Me for wisdom and knowledge that you might govern My people over whom I have made you king, wisdom and knowledge are now given to you. Possessions, wealth, and honor I will also give to you; such has not been given to kings before you nor those who will follow after you."
>
> —2 CHRONICLES 1:11–12, MEV

Take a moment to ponder this. We were designed by God with the capacity to not simply commune with Him through conversation but be one with God—to share His thoughts and perceptions, to know His mind through His Spirit. When Adam and Eve walked with God in the cool of the morning, they didn't always need the verbal communication that so limits humanity now. They had an inner communication pathway through their connectedness to Him.

No man since Adam had asked God for connection on this level, and Adam hadn't even asked for it; he was created with it. Solomon was not just asking to be wise like the Sunday school teachers tell us; he was asking to be reconnected to the *šāmaʿ*, the Hebrew word for sharing the same headspace with God, or to share God's intelligence, wisdom, and perceptions.[1]

This is a key principle in this story. Solomon's request excited God because it was His very real, original intention to commune with mankind in this way, and this is why He gave Solomon so much, because Solomon was being radically realigned with God's original design and plan. God was making a statement here, saying, "If you want to be connected to Me and My mind, everything will follow that—all wealth, power, and authority." This was the very first time God made such a point of this, and it would be the last time He would do so on this level until Jesus came and demonstrated in an even greater way what it means to be connected to the mind of God. Then we also received the potential to experience this through Christ.

As I watched Solomon stand after this encounter with God, he had changed. It wasn't that he had been transformed or given superhuman intelligence. He had been wired rightly so that he could perceive what was in the master builder's thoughts and emotions. He was tapping into the wisdom and intelligence of God—not like someone using a superpower but out of sonship—and He was sharing God's thoughts, emotions, and even intentions. He was inspired from within, not just governed by a spiritual being from without. Solomon was flowing in tune with a loving God who was showing humanity what was possible through His connection to him. This was a new day for humanity.

This picture of divine enlightenment drives whole economies in the religious world, but it was freely given to Solomon to do with God the work that He intended. God wanted His people to be able to receive His love through the leadership and wisdom Solomon displayed. This alignment drove Solomon to build a city that surrounded a great temple and behind it a palace so beautiful, so extravagant, that the world had never experienced the like before.

A Vision Within a Vision

The angel with me let me see that clusters of living neuropathways from God's mind in heaven were overlapping Solomon's. As I looked deeply into one cluster, which looked like roots of a plant, I had a vision within my vision. I could see that the temple and the design Solomon was creating imitated the design of the Garden of Eden.

In my vision the innermost place Solomon created was called the holy of holies, but in the spirit I could see that this inner holy place was overlapped by the tree of life in the garden. The design of the temple was symbolic of God's intention to restore us to complete connection with Him. Isn't it amazing that the man who had the closest connection to God up to this point in time was developing a symbolic and religious structure that would enable man to reenter God's intended place of connection, at least through ritual? This whole temple structure was such a shadow, such a hidden message, for the people of Israel (and for the whole world) of what was to come.

I could see the holy of holies leading into the next room, the holy place, which led out to the outer courts. Through these sections, God was creating through Solomon (and previously through other temple worship) the symbolism of a spiritual journey back to the Garden of Eden.

I didn't know this at the time, but I learned much later that, symbolically, the priests for the children of Israel would go into the temple and retrace the steps past the cherubim in a westward direction, depicting the return to the garden. The outer courts represented the fallen world, while the inner court represented a holier way of life that the priests passed into, but only the high priest could enter the holy of all holies. Similarly, Adam and Eve were cast out to the east, and cherubim guarded the garden, preventing them from reentry.

Spiritually, Solomon's architectural design became a symbolic picture of our realignment to the garden and our reconnection to God. He did what no one could do up until him, and he did it in a way that the Bible declares was never rivaled.

After the temple was built, can you imagine how many people came as tourists—from the entire known world—just to see the marvel of the people whose God loved them? Can you imagine what they thought as they saw how God was leading His people through a king who had shaped every part of the way they lived with wisdom unlike anything anyone had ever experienced? It was probably a little like experiencing heaven touching earth.

The temple and Solomon's leadership were also a messianic vision of what was to come, or, to put it another way, it was one of the ways God built anticipation in the Israelites for their promised Savior. Through Solomon they saw God as a kingdom shaper, a builder of heaven on earth, someone who could bring Israel peace and connection to the world around them while reigning with a power bar none. It was all so different from a barbarian way of being led.

Solomon's messianic example was also one of the main reasons the first people who followed Jesus were confused. They expected Him to come with natural guidance and kingdom-building ways first, not begin with an internal rebirth.

Solomon accumulated even more wealth after his alignment with God, and his leadership had no rival. In my vision I could see trade routes opening that were forbidden in David's time because David had been at war with those countries. Solomon declared peace on all sides but protected the peace of God and His people with wisdom, not with political strategies.

Once the city was built, the whole world gathered there. Kings and queens came from afar and offered tribute to a God they had never imagined worshipping. The Israelites were no longer at war. They had so much of God's favor on them that people from everywhere visited in the hope it would rub off on them. They also came to learn from all the modern technology, city building, and worship they would see and experience.

But what I was seeing was only the beginning.

CHAPTER 2

TO HAVE THE PERCEPTIONS OF GOD

WHAT I SAW next shocked me. The vision fast-forwarded again. I went from Israel—overlooking Solomon and having the awesome experience of watching him cry out to God for oneness of mind and heart so he could rule God's people—to something I would not have expected.

I saw us—you and me.

Solomon was the first to cry out for something that God had always intended we have. It was how we were all made to be: connected and divinely intelligent so we could live the greater life that is supernatural and super-empowered, the John 10:10 life that Jesus offered when He said, "I came that they may have and enjoy life, and have it in abundance [to the full, till it overflows]" (AMP). This is a life abundantly more than anything you have seen.

In the vision I saw us, and I saw God breathing on us. This reality, the divine connection and alignment that Solomon had, was for us as well, and even more!

I also saw the Father answering Jesus' cry the night before He died, when He prayed that we would be one with Him, just as He and the Father are one; that we would be perfected and completed into one; and that we would be with Him where He is (John 17:21, 24). What God intended all along—a restoration to oneness in the garden—was offered to us again after the atonement, after what Jesus did on the cross.

During this vision my mind made a huge departure from a religious mindset, and I opened up certain scriptures and read them as if they were brand-new. The Spirit of God showed me how Paul was able to clearly articulate the profound reality of our connection to God in 1 Corinthians 2. Most Christians discount it as poetry or look at it as just something from the past that only Paul's generation of Christians had access to, but the Spirit told me that the closer we get to Jesus' return, the more this passage will define what Christianity could look like if we accessed the same kind of relationship with God. Paul laid it out the clearest in 1 Corinthians 2:10–16:

> God now unveils these profound realities to us by the Spirit. Yes, he has revealed to us his inmost heart and deepest mysteries through the Holy Spirit, who constantly explores all things. After all, who can really see into a person's heart and know his hidden impulses except for that person's spirit? So it is with God. His thoughts and secrets are only fully understood by his Spirit, the Spirit of God.
>
> For we did not receive the spirit of this world system but the Spirit of God, so that we might come to understand and experience all that grace has lavished upon us. And we articulate these realities with the words imparted to us by the Spirit and not with the words taught by human wisdom. We join together Spirit-revealed truths with Spirit-revealed words. Someone living on an entirely human level rejects the revelations of God's Spirit, for they make no sense to him. He can't understand the revelations of the Spirit because they are only discovered by the illumination of the Spirit. Those

who live in the Spirit are able to carefully evaluate all things, and they are subject to the scrutiny of no one but God.

For who has ever intimately known the mind of the Lord Yahweh well enough to become his counselor? *Christ has,* and we possess Christ's perceptions.

We were created to share Christ's perceptions of everything He has created, to co-labor with Him to work and govern His creation. He never designed us to work externally from Him as power brokers of a resource but rather internally—where the joy of the experience comes from doing it *with* Him, not *for* Him.

Jesus clearly laid this out when He explained how the connection He prophesied to the disciples in John 14, 15, and 16 would work. He said He was leaving but that One would come, called His Spirit or the Spirit of God, who would relate the Father's will to us.

Let's look at those exact passages to get a feel for this process because this way of communing with God is exactly what we are entitled to, and it will change everything.

> Loving me empowers you to obey my commands. And I will ask the Father and he will give you another Savior, the Holy Spirit of Truth, who will be to you a friend just like me—and he will never leave you. The world won't receive him because they can't see him or know him. But you know him intimately because he remains with you and will live inside you.
>
> —JOHN 14:15–16

> I will send you the Divine Encourager from the very presence of my Father. He will come to you, the Spirit of Truth, emanating from the Father, and he will speak to you about me. And you will tell everyone the truth about me, for you have walked with me from the start.
>
> —JOHN 15:26–27

There is so much more I would like to say to you, but it's more than you can grasp at this moment. But when the truth-giving Spirit comes, he will unveil the reality of every truth within you. He won't speak on his own, but only what he hears from the Father, and he will reveal prophetically to you what is to come. He will glorify me on the earth, for he will receive from me what is mine and reveal it to you. Everything that belongs to the Father belongs to me—that's why I say that the Divine Encourager will receive what is mine and reveal it to you. Soon you won't see me any longer, but then, after a little while, you will see me in a new way.

—JOHN 16:12–16

Jesus promised that we will have His Spirit abiding in us to connect us to God. While on earth not only was Jesus developing a heart of obedience and love—so that we could all be like messianic versions of Solomon or Joseph, Daniel or Esther; He was also creating a context of faith for how we are built to share the Father's mind, heart, and affections. The things Joseph, Daniel, and Esther did were shaped by sharing God's thoughts and perceptions in the world. Joseph navigated government with revelation. Daniel occupied a pagan kingdom from the inside, bringing transformation and protection for his people. Esther was brought into a position of favor and power to bring God's love and redemption on His people. We will do what they did in the natural world, but we will also be empowered by this promised inner connection to God.

THE VISION OF NEURONS FROM HEAVEN

The next vision in this series of encounters came to me during a business consulting meeting. I was listening to a chairman talk about a new idea for his company, and as he talked, I saw through the Spirit of God his neurons firing and lighting up his mind like Christmas tree lights. It was an explosion of mental activity. As I kept looking, I saw what looked to be the greatest, most beautiful brain—God's mind—overlapping his, and I knew I was seeing the Father's thoughts and brilliance at work.

Then it was like I was sucked in and riding on the chairman's neural pathways. As I did, I was absorbing his thoughts, his intelligence, and his emotions. I was shot like water through the root system of his neuro network, and it felt like both a ride and an invasion of brilliance in my own being.

I couldn't fathom what I was seeing, feeling, or experiencing. It was so exciting and overwhelming. As I rode by, I kept getting these glimpses of neurons that resembled thought bubbles. Was that the blueprint for a new automobile harnessing energy in a way we had never discovered before? Was that a computer installed to work alongside the human mind to create connections to technology that we have never seen? Was that a new water system for farms in drought areas? Was that a thought about how to infuse our cells with oxygen to delay our DNA's aging process? Was that inspiration for a cure for cancer?

Thousands of these neurons were firing, and each one was cleverer than the previous one. Some neurons were so advanced that I only understood them while I was in that place; they were too advanced for me to even relate to when I came out of the vision. I saw technologies for printing cells, food, even DNA; technologies for space travel and occupying other planets; technologies to change world currencies and banking. I don't want to sound like the ideas were sci-fi, but there is so much unthought of and undiscovered that will come.

As I rode around between God's neurology and this man's, I seemed to land again in the space between heaven and earth right when the team I was meeting with asked me for spiritual insight into what they were discussing with me, so I shared some things. Then they told me about a new transportation company they were starting that was so outside of the box I can't even talk about it yet. The idea for it was inspired only because God had taken them on a spiritual life journey—He gave them signs to direct them and the faith to obey—and they were trying to reconstruct the space they were working within with His redemptive technology and desire. The idea was straight out of what I was seeing in the vision—the result of them sharing in the vastness of God's creative thinking.

I was dizzy with both what I had seen and what the team was sharing. My mind had expanded times ten but only briefly. As I was coming out of this vision, I was stripped of the brilliance of what I had seen. My mind, however, was imprinted with the awesomeness of it, and ever since, I've had a hunger to build a connection into inviting the Holy Spirit to help me experience the perceptions of Christ and the Father.

The Scriptures say, "Things never discovered or heard of before, things beyond our ability to imagine—these are the many things God has in store for all his lovers. But God now unveils these profound realities to us by the Spirit" (1 Cor. 2:9–10).

WE HAVE A BIBLICAL PROTOTYPE IN SOLOMON

Solomon asked for what God had always intended, and when he received it, it caused Israel's transformation. It changed the city structure, it caused governmental alignment in the nations around Israel, and it brought social and economic justice and prosperity.

Solomon, even with the wisdom and experience he inherited from his father, King David, would never have been able to build what he did without having a continuous connection to God's mind. I think many people thought he was just infused with the power of wisdom, but he wrote in the Book of Proverbs about the *persona* of wisdom—that the kind of wisdom that comes from God is part of who God is. God's wisdom comes out of connection to Him; it's not an infusion of something that is detached from Him.

In my vision I saw us sharing God's mind and seeing the same results as Solomon. When you are around brilliant people—and I have been privileged to be around some truly brilliant minds—the process of how they live life, do what they are gifted for, and express their talents rubs off on you. Their brilliance creates a glory around them, and you benefit from it.

The prophet Isaiah said the Spirit that God promised would rest on the Messiah (Isaiah 11) is personified in seven ways. "The Spirit of Yahweh will rest upon him, the Spirit of Extraordinary Wisdom, the Spirit of Perfect Understanding the Spirit of Wise Strategy, the Spirit of Mighty Power, the Spirit of Revelation, and the Spirit of the Fear of Yahweh" (Isa. 11:2).

We see this again in the Book of Revelation: "The first voice I heard was like a trumpet speaking with me, saying, 'Come up here, and I will show you things which must take place after this.'…Seven lamps of fire were burning before the throne, which are the seven Spirits of God" (Rev. 4:1, 5, MEV).

These seven spirits are part of the atmosphere and inner culture God carries. When we are around Him, connected to Him, these get empowered within our own spirit. Our spirit could be seen as a plug, and we are plugging in to the power source of His nature.

1. The Spirit of the Lord

2. The Spirit of wisdom

3. The Spirit of understanding

4. The Spirit of counsel

5. The Spirit of strength

6. The Spirit of knowledge

7. The Spirit of the fear of the Lord

These were *and are* the seven main parts of God's spiritual operating system. They were all the same qualities you would see in someone ordained for government and rulership.

Jesus prophesied that the same seven-spirit nature of God will operate in us to bring us this connection. I don't think most Christians are consumed with bringing the Spirit of wise strategy or the Spirit of mighty power into situations, but that is exactly what the world is crying out for. The world is looking for people who are other than normal. They are looking for a relationship with God to add a value that *nothing* else can add. That is exactly what Isaiah prophesied over the Messiah in Isaiah 11, and we watched Jesus walk out an earthly life of bringing connection, solutions, disruptions, and counsel to the world around Him in ways that were *unexpected and unbelievable.*

Solomon was one of the first messianic prototypes of building God's kingdom on earth with God's wisdom. When Jesus came, He didn't build this in the natural sense; He came to deliver to us these seven keys so that we could build the kingdom with and through Him. Christ reconnected and re-empowered us, and now our job is to manifest the wisdom of God in every quadrant of society and over everything man has dominion over.

Even if this sounds radical on this side of eternity, this *will be* our reality after Jesus' return. God designed us, through our relationship with Him, to manifest His love in ways that shape the world around us—not just through evangelism but by populating the earth with God's original intention and strategy.

I love what Solomon's dad's best friend, Hiram, wrote after Solomon asked him for a skilled craftsman and timber for the temple.

> Then Hiram king of Tyre responded in a letter that he sent to Solomon, "Because the Lord loves His people, He has made you king over them." And Hiram said, "Blessed be the Lord God

of Israel who made heaven and earth and has given King David a wise son, having insight and understanding."

—2 CHRONICLES 2:11–12, MEV

In other words, the love of God was displayed for His people in the way Solomon demonstrated it—through his rulership, influence, and practical building of grace on the earth.

The world is waiting to see the love of God manifest, to see the land healed, to see Christians begin to see God's desire for the nations, to see the kind of love that God sent His only Son, Jesus, to bridge us to. This love has tangible metrics, and we see that play out in the most powerful way for the nation of Israel during Solomon's reign.

In my vision about sharing the innermost thoughts and perceptions of the Father, having the mind of Christ through our spiritual rebirth was connected directly to something else I saw.

THE BRANDED ONES

I saw a branding on the hearts of people who are being called right now. It was based on a scripture that is also a key for now.

> When I shut up the heaven and there is no rain, or when I command the locusts to devour the land, or send pestilence on My people, if My people, who are called by My name, will humble themselves and pray, and seek My face and turn from their wicked ways, then I will hear from heaven, and will forgive their sin and will heal their land. Now My eyes will be open and My ears attentive to the prayer of this place. So now I have chosen and consecrated this house that My name be there continually. *My eyes and heart will be there for all days.*
>
> —2 CHRONICLES 7:13–16, MEV, EMPHASIS ADDED

This isn't just a scriptural text that gives us prayer points. This is the position that we need to live from. We must open our hearts and believe that God's goals are our goals, not the other way around. We are *not* going to set the goal of using *our* gifts, talents, and strengths *for* God, nor will we just carry out our destiny and mission based on *our* wisdom and knowledge.

God's words are for a people who humble themselves and realize that the problems with world hunger and morality, the attack against the nuclear family, and the issues over governments and nations are not natural issues but spiritual ones. The only way we can see the metrics change is by humbling ourselves and calling on God, who we know can heal our land and cleanse our sin.

A modern way to say it is that we need to open our whole being to God and acknowledge that we don't have the capacity to change anyone or anything without Him. And as we realize the bankruptcy of ourselves and the world around us without God, we embrace the free gift of what He is giving: the *sōzō*, or salvation,[1] that isn't a onetime occurrence but a lifestyle that creates an authority to do things not just *for* God but *with* God.

I love when Paul talks because he's a straight shooter. He explained this lifestyle to the Corinthians when he said, "The message I preached and how I preached it was not an attempt to sway you with persuasive arguments but to prove to you the almighty power of God's Holy Spirit. For God intended that your faith not be established on man's wisdom but by trusting in his almighty power" (1 Cor. 2:4–5). Another word for God's power, *dynamis*, refers to the inherent power in God by virtue of His nature.[2] And Paul followed this with his description of exactly how we are connected to the mind of God (vv. 6–16).

Solomon's life on this side of eternity was based on a model. Paul explained it as God's plan for how we can see Him transform culture and lives. He said that God's eyes will be open and His ears attentive to the prayers offered in this place of connection (v. 15). You have to understand, we are not just His hands and feet displaying His nature in the midst of the trouble in the world around us; we are also His eyes and ears. He is going to move *His* compassion through human vessels. He is going to give *His* wisdom and strategy, *His* business and city models, *His* kingdom-shaping abilities *to people whom He can give eyes and ears to*—and He won't just rest upon us; He will cohabit with us through the Spirit.

You are made to be His dwelling place, and His eyes and ears are seeing and listening to you even now, day and night.

What does this vision and perspective mean practically? It means that the spiritual and mental enlightenment the world is so longing to "attain" is one of the main benefits God intended His children to have! Sharing God's mind is not just an empowering of information and wisdom, being one with the fundamental wisdom of all the universe. It's a oneness found only in a spiritual relationship with God the Creator—His original intention and design based on that relationship between Him and us, as well as between us and the world around us. God shaped us in a way that when we plug in to Him, we fit like a glove. We were perfectly made for Him.

God sent Jesus to restore this relationship and design, and Jesus gave us the keys to manifest it. These keys, unlike in Solomon's day, were not to just build a natural kingdom or society, or even the temple for the Israelites. The keys we were given, the ones Jesus apprehended for us, are keys to restore humanity and then bring the world forward into the rule and reign of our King.

This is an end-time message. We are called to see with His eyes, hear with His ears, and perceive with His thoughts. Everything is accelerating right now. More and more people are being called— like Solomons in their spheres of influence, careers, societies—to be able to not just think with excellence but think like God and to perceive *His* solutions to spiritually and naturally rooted issues.

Encountering God doesn't make us so heavenly minded that we aren't any earthly good. It actually causes us to see the shape and form of what He intended, and even now intends, in the world around us. We get to become builders of His marvelous kingdom, a kingdom that is equally and outstandingly practical and spiritual.

CHAPTER 3

BEING ROOTED INTO GOD'S PLAN

RIGHT AFTER THESE visions, I was on a movie set for a day, and the director had chosen the location because it had both practical sets and facades. A facade is a structure that is only a shell or a face of a building. When actors are standing in front of it, it looks real, but it is hollow inside. Practical sets are more realistic—they are actual buildings with rooms you can enter or exit.

Production companies use facades because they are easier to build and better on the budget; often only one or two scenes are being filmed in a particular setting, and there's no need for a detailed set because most of it won't be seen. Practical sets are used when actors are filmed going from one part of the set to another and the filmmaker wants to present more of a fluid experience. Sometimes you can't tell the difference as a viewer, but most actors I know love to be immersed in a more realistic environment. On a practical set the actors don't have to try as hard or pull on as much acting skill because they can easily picture themselves in the realm of the story.

When I was on this set, I had a vision that felt like a

continuation of this prophetic message God was building in me. I saw a young Christian boy reading a book about the earth. In it he was being told that it was fake and not what God really intended and that it would be passing away soon—when Jesus returned.

Then I realized I was that little boy, and that is what I had been taught. In our generation many Christians have been told that the earth is a facade—it's not real and will pass away. Most Christians treat this beautiful place where God Himself rested on the seventh day after He created it as if it is destined to burn up and has no practical value. The vast majority of Christians think they will be going to live in a city in heaven and that the earth will be destroyed or that they are going to build a new earth, and even a new heaven, with Jesus. This has been our belief system for quite some time, and there are several big reasons this has been imparted from one generation to the next. But it just isn't true.

We see that after the fall of man the earth immediately started dying too, so we are ready to bury it and move on. Most of us don't have a love for this earth because of a mindset that we are merely pilgrims on our way somewhere else. Yes, there are many songs written about this, and a few scriptures taken out of context will make us feel this way. Those who seem to love the earth are often seen by other Christians as worldly or carnal—we have dualized what is spiritual and practical, calling all practical reality carnal or fleshly and everything else spiritual.

Paul, the greatest teacher of the Christian faith, went to great lengths to keep us from coming under such beliefs, but here we are, two thousand years later, and we are still misunderstanding what is fleshly, carnal, or sinful and what is natural. Natural and carnal are two completely different things.

- What is natural can actually be covered with God's glory.

- What is carnal is separate from God and kills our ability to relate to Jesus.

When we have the wrong theology about the earth, thinking it's going to be destroyed, we are operating in direct conflict with the fundamental biblical nature of God. He created the whole earth and everything in it to be a place that is full of His glory, and by stewarding it with Him, we can experience the depth of His nature and love, which are all around us.

This whole thing started in the garden in the middle of the earth. We are designed to be gardeners, walking with God to steward something so complex, so original, that it just might take an eternity to keep developing it, based on what we have found to be true in science so far.

God always intended redemption and renewal, not destruction. He even made a final claim on this truth through His death and resurrection. Jesus died on a tree, much like the tree of the knowledge of good and evil we stole from, to restore us to the tree of life. Have you ever thought about the prophetic picture seen in the fact that when Mary saw a man standing by the empty tomb, she mistook Him for a gardener? This was the start of our journey back to the original Garden of Eden. Jesus was the new Adam, and He did not strip the trees and eat from them for His own vanity, nor did He hide from God; He boldly announced the *new* way.

THE POINTS OF LIGHT BLANKETING THE EARTH

In one of my earlier visions, which I outlined in *Keys to Heaven's Economy*, I was hovering above the earth on a dark night and saw all of these points of light on the earth. They represented solo believers or companies of believers, such as organizations or churches. Then, as God was inspiring relational connection among them, the points of light began to join in the form of friendships and business relationships that would engage divine purpose, and it looked like a net of light was covering the earth.

So many people who have read about this or heard me share it have told me through the years that they saw the same vision, and they were so encouraged. It came with the Scripture reference of John 17—Jesus' own prayer. Jesus prayed that we would be one as He is one, and it is this unity that is the currency of God moving on the earth. There will be disunity in every sector of the world, even in religious structures that are not directly connected to relational practice with God, but those who are walking with God can walk in His unity. We are wired to unite and build, no matter how different we are. You can't expect that what Jesus prayed for and paid such a sacrificial price for would be rendered void or in default. The Father fully intends to release unity and, on top of that, the heavenly blessing that flows on the earth only through our united connections.

THE SECOND VERSION OF THE VISION OF CONNECTED LIGHTS

I saw this vision again a few years later, only this time when the points of light were joined, they looked like the root system of a vast tree. Above this root system was a giant oak, and it was so colossal it put the sequoias to shame.

> I am sent to announce a new season of Yahweh's grace and a time of God's recompense on his enemies, to comfort all who are in sorrow, to strengthen those crushed by despair who mourn in Zion—to give them a beautiful bouquet in the place of ashes, the oil of bliss instead of tears, and the mantle of joyous praise instead of the spirit of heaviness. Because of

this, they will be known as *Mighty Oaks of Righteousness,* planted by Yahweh as a *living* display of his glory.

— ISAIAH 61:2–3, EMPHASIS ADDED

When you look at this passage, you see that God was going to strengthen Zion and the children of Israel in a time of oppression, at a time when they were robbed. We see the turning of the circumstances and the tools God was going to bring to strengthen and redeem the situations. You also see what the Lord called them in the time of redemption: Mighty Oaks of Righteousness.

Humanity has a very special reverence for oak trees. The oak tree has been an important symbol to a variety of cultures through many centuries. Germany and England have named it their national tree because of its great strength.[1] In 2004 the oak also was named the national tree of the United States.[2] Oak trees can live hundreds of years, which explains why they often symbolize endurance.

I once read that in ancient Greek and Roman civilizations, wearing oak leaves signified royalty and conferred a special status. In the US military, oak leaf clusters are a symbol of honor on awards. Some also consider the acorn, the seed of the oak tree, a significant symbol of unlimited potential because something so small can grow into such a big, strong tree.[3]

The Bible uses the picture of a tree in prophetic promises for the people of God and even in communicating our identity. We read about a follower of God "standing firm like a flourishing tree planted by God's design" (Ps. 1:3), offering "others fruit from the tree of life" (Prov. 15:4), and being a "healing tree of life to those who taste her fruits" (Prov. 3:18). Jeremiah 17 gives us a powerful amplification of what Isaiah 61 presents: "Blessed is the man who trusts in the Lord, and whose hope is the Lord. For he shall be as a tree planted by the waters, and that spreads out its roots by the river, and shall not fear when heat comes, but its leaf shall be green, and it shall not be anxious in the year of drought, neither shall cease from yielding fruit" (vv. 7–8, MEV).

I realized my vision symbolized two things:

1. A lot of what God has been doing in planting Christians in His incredible purpose has been underground, or just below the surface of what we can see, when we look at world issues, problems, and people. He has been planting seeds that are now maturing. They have a healthy root system and are about to come to the surface.

2. God is rooting us into cultures all over the world. What is down below in their root system is a rich expression of beautiful faith that is about to bear fruit on the surface of every culture.

Right after I saw this vision, I was at a conference with one of my spiritual friends named Bob Jones, who was so good at interpreting these things. I was about to tell him the vision when he prophesied to me, "God is going to use you to raise up oaks of righteousness!"

"Unbelievable," I thought. Bob confirmed exactly what I had been seeing in my spirit before I'd said a word.

We had just moved to Los Angeles, and Bob began to prophesy about the relocation: "I see the land of LA, and just below the surface is an interlocking network of a bad root system that is producing terrible fruit for the nations. God is about to break up this root system, and when He does, He is going to plant people like you there to be a righteous root. You will help to develop a root system that will bring fruit to feed the nations through arts, entertainment, and media." He quoted Proverbs 12:3 (MEV): "A man will not be established by wickedness, but the root of the righteous will not be moved."

"I see you raising up the oaks of righteousness!" he said again.

I was overwhelmed because through Bob's word I understood the huge vision I'd had of what God was doing through the righteous root system Bob described.

As Bob spoke about entertainment and media, I knew he was talking about things that had been wrongly empowered and locked down in so many of these industries. At the time, Christians could hardly even have space there, but it was powerful that what Bob was sharing sounded almost the same as the vision I'd had but applied to me.

A New Root System

Then Bob went further and said, "When God gives you a miracle house in LA, it will be a sign that you will be planted like a seed and that a new network of roots of believers is forming in entertainment and media. And when you get a house in LA, from that time on you will see many building miracles, and many people you are involved with will also get miracle properties. This will represent God rooting you into His purposes and creating that new, righteous root system."

That was so profound to me and to our spiritual family. I was able to share it with believers throughout LA. It is *so* hard to get housing, business, workspace, and entertainment space without a large sum of money in LA, so we knew that for what God was showing us to manifest, we would need miracles. For me, it wasn't just about the buildings but about this vision of God rooting Christians into the fabric of His spiritual purposes for the earth so that we would begin to enter into a time of restoration. Even in real estate culture, they talk about owning land and how having housing roots you into your city.

The Root System Going In

In 2016 we experienced a miracle in Studio City. It is such a big story it would take its own book to give all the details. We were able to get a miraculous property that was truly one of a kind—it included a soundstage, house, guest house, and a mixed-use workspace.

Within twelve months of getting our property in 2016, we had dozens of friends get housing and space for their projects, businesses, and ministries. Before this, maybe one or two friends, businesses, or entertainment groups had been able to buy property each year, and now suddenly we were seeing a mini landslide of property ownership.

It was a pretty significant time for us. Up until then, buying property was one of our biggest community struggles because of the cost of living in LA. The year 2016 was a real tipping point, and we saw it as the realization of this word from Bob Jones. Now we are seeing that this word is being fulfilled in layers—for us, locally, growing roots in the form of property, but also for God's oaks of righteousness growing roots and heavenly networks or relational connections in cultures around the world.

The Roots Coming Out of You

I have traveled a lot in my life, but since 2016 I have been inundated with stories of people who are getting placed in positions of authority. They are newly able to leverage their work and careers for kingdom purposes, and they are having great influence in cultural and marketplace issues. I started podcasts just to capture some of the stories that can be told publicly, but the most powerful ones will not be able to be told in this lifetime because of their sensitive nature.

I will talk about the other encounters that add to this heavenly perspective, but I want to share an encounter from 2020 here. During the global pandemic, I started to see visions of fields of mature trees. I saw these fields over and over but had not connected them to the root system visions. I just wasn't thinking with my spiritual mind about it, yet I kept seeing the mature trees that will be a theme throughout this book.

Then we had another life miracle happen that my family and I weren't even looking for. My wife found a property in a part of LA we had never looked at before, in the foothills of some of LA's mountains. We both knew that we knew we were supposed to purchase it, even though it meant giving up our miracle property from four years before. The thing about this property was that it held dozens of mature, protected oak trees. The people who lived there before us even had an organization that had "oaks" in its name, and they were Christians as well. This was a house God had promised them that had been prayed over. We moved into a true promised land that is totally set up for this phase of our purpose, and historic, old oak trees are its marking feature.

I believe the root system in my visions is being established for the next move of God, and we are already seeing the trees that are growing up and out of it, which are about to bear fruit. I also have had a recurring vision when I meet people or see old friends—I see a lit-up rooted system coming out of them, and I know it represents that they are becoming ready for their greater purpose.

One more thing to note here is that at about ten events I was hosting or speaking at in 2019, which had crowds of seven hundred or more, I asked how many people had recently dreamed of oak trees. There were thirty to 150 in each crowd. I don't think this is coincidence. God is raising something up—and using biblical language for it—in one of the most historic moves of His Spirit in our generation and beyond.

CHAPTER 4

GOD'S ORIGINAL DESIGN

I N MY NEXT encounter in this series of visitations, I was in a dreamlike vision, and everything around me was very hard to understand. Was I standing inside the most beautiful painting come to life? Was I somehow living inside the melody of the most majestic song? Where was I?

"You are seeing the *before*," came a voice from somewhere next to me. I didn't understand the angel's words, but I was experiencing a euphoria that made me feel as if every one of my cells was vibrating with God's glory.

After a while, in a subsequent parabolic vision, God allowed me to see the Trinity—Father, Son, and Holy Spirit—and they seemed to be sitting around a table, but everything was a little blurry, almost as if I wasn't supposed to be able to see in fullness.

We were up in an area that felt like clouds; there was rain and lightning, but the area felt very soft and harmless. "This place is the firmament from where God hovered over everything He created," the angel said.

I noticed Jesus the most. Thank God I couldn't fully see Him. He was so breathtakingly overwhelming I would have felt as if I was going to die if I had. He held something almost like a 3D holo-gram in His hand, and it was in the shape of a human being. He said, "Look at this one. Can you imagine what she will do when she discovers what we have put inside of her? Isn't she awesome?" He slammed His other hand on the table and jumped up.

The Father laughed a bellowing laugh. It wasn't like Santa's laugh; it was beyond jolly. He found so much joy in Jesus' fascina-tion and love for this human.

"You have said that about all of them," He said.

Behind the Father and Jesus were billions of these 3D images of humans, hanging by beautiful strings. I looked for the end of the strings, and it made me emotional to see that the strings were intermeshed with the Father's heart. They were part of Him—found in the deepest part of His core.

The holograms were brilliant with light. Jesus grabbed another and held it up among the three of them, and they all communed and imagined and planned over the person. They planned the person's identity, joy, gender, and physical form; the individual's relationship capacity; then his or her talents, skills, imagination and dream life, and potential. So much care and creative expres-sion went into this process. I was seeing the artists of all artisans at work, and it felt so holy.

Then they did something that felt extremely holy, and I watched the three of them carefully install something of their own will and imagination into the person.

"There it is." Jesus grinned.

The Father let His hand wander over the heart of the person, who wasn't alive yet but was fully alive in His imagination.

The angel next to me whispered, "They just predestined their image, nature, and purpose." His quiet words hung in the air.

Even though it was the most fascinating thing I had ever watched—the Godhead dreaming of a human and molding Their nature into this tiny vessel—it felt like eternity was flying by. I looked at some of the spirits of the men and women I could see close to me and realized they each had the equivalent of millions of years, or the Godhead's own eternity, go into their creative process. They were formed in the imagination of God and brought into their potential existence. It was breathtaking.

As they all passed around the person they were working on, I could see their imaginations, dreams, and desires carefully writing the DNA of the person they held. Have you ever seen a master-piece by a famous artist? Can you imagine watching a time-lapse of their artistic process? We get to see that sometimes, in a minor way, through social media, but this was such artistry that no one in the world could see this and fully understand what God Himself put into humanity, this intricate planning of how His image could inspire and bring forth another person, who would be a unique expression of who He is.

"*Ohhhhhh*, my favorite part!" Jesus shouted over the one they worked on. They were writing into the very nature of the person how she would express and receive love. "She will love the way we love." And as He said that, Jesus was breathing His nature into the fabric of her natural and spiritual being. He was building her anticipation for romance and a husband. He was stirring within her the desire to reproduce. He was writing on her spirit the ability to produce resources and work hard. She was a powerful, strong leader, and I saw His joy about that strength; it was like He had reserved something of a ferocity for her, but it was tempered by her nurturing heart for those she loved.

Color filled the sky, and it looked like the lightning bolts of heaven were shooting all around. It was the greatest light display I had ever seen. These lights seemed to have a target, and they focused it into her. It was the Holy Spirit's turn to work, and when the power of the Spirit anointed her, it was like nothing I had ever seen.

I thought, "Surely she must have a destiny to be a giant leader in the world," because the creative power of God's nature was soaking her in brilliance and sticking to every fiber of her being. She was the most awesome person I'd ever seen. *Wow*! Was I seeing a modern-day Mother Teresa being formed? Was this woman a leader in God's end-time army? Surely she was one for the history books.

Two things shone brighter than almost anything else that He put in her. I thought, "What are those?"

The angel next to me, who was just beyond my vision, answered, "On her earthly side of eternity, these two things you are seeing are her ability to nurture relationships and her ability to share resources. She will do both out of a place that is so sacrificial it may be the only way that some of the people she encounters will ever know this love she was made with."

Then I had a vision of her life on earth, and I was distressed. She was being born into pretty harsh poverty. I was wounded over the vision and that the nature of God inside her seemed so limited in her natural life. "How can she carry so much of God, and yet this is her earthly story? How can this woman, who I thought would be a Joan of Arc on the earth, be a mother born in the slums who has virtually nothing?" I could not understand this at all.

"You are seeing her after the result of sin," the angel said. "Not only is the image and nature of God inside her disconnected, but by the time you are seeing this vision, it has been so for generations."

It grieved me, and I mourned for her. There was so much injustice in the fall. The Godhead seemed aware of all I was seeing, but They stayed unhindered by it; they created each person with as much passion as if mankind would never make that fateful decision in the garden.

The World Champion

I watched them grab another hologram. This one was a man who felt very familiar to me. I knew he must have been born in my generation. I saw his capacity for partnering in marriage, being a father, being a leader, and excelling with these incredible gifts God was wrapping around his very identity. He was glorious! God's glory lined the inside of him.

Then I watched him being born. He was born to a mother who loved him but a father who was extremely detached. Even in his birth, I could see the disconnection in his family that would wreak havoc on God's glorious image inside of him and on his potential.

He had a hard upbringing, living in total poverty with uneducated parents who divorced. He, however, had that brilliant, strategic mind that God put inside of him, and he was always looking for ways to become better.

He married a woman, his first wife, and she was a catalyst for his completeness, but he never really loved her as much as he loved success and himself. She worked part-time to help support the home while he followed his entrepreneurial dreams of success.

At this stage, the angel next to me looked sad. "He is using what has been put inside of him, that inner glory of God's nature, to try and fulfill an identity that is a bottomless pit without connection to the Creator. He will work himself to the death of all relationships, even with the children he will have with his second wife."

I watched it play out—three marriages, several children who desperately wanted to be loved by him but were sacrificed at the altar of ambition, and success that was valued only by the world around him. But heaven was hovering over him, still pregnant with God's original dream, still holding him to that. Heaven was trying to interject opportunities for him to slow down and see Jesus: in the role of father as he held his baby for the first time, in the role of husband, which could have been an eternal picture of life but instead had become an issue of convenience to him.

Then he was old and slightly bitter. One of his grandchildren had found Jesus and become a minister and came to visit him. The grandson was so happy, so full of life, so detached from the natural ambition that had defined the man's own success and glory, and somehow the simplicity of his grandson's life with his small family melted the man's heart. He finally saw what he had somehow avoided: he saw the life that was truly life. He felt too old to apprehend it, though, and I could see hopelessness and complacency over him. His grandson and family were going to a church meeting in his town on the last night of their visit, and they invited him. He hadn't been to a church meeting in years. He considered himself a Christian, but only in theory, because in his field it was the respectable choice when people asked your religion.

There I was on the stage ministering, sharing about the love of God and hearing His voice. It was on one of my tour stops back in 2017. It was surreal, watching myself and seeing this man in the audience. I was sharing my guts out. I actually remembered this time and city, and more memories flooded back to me. This had already happened in my earthly life, but I had no awareness of this man until the *me* onstage began to prophesy to him.

I prophesied a simple word: "God has made you a powerful family man, and the way He wants you to give and receive love is in the context of your grandkids and kids. You will help their dreams come true with your resources, and they will help your dreams come true by what they do, which will so inspire you."

It was a very general word in so many ways, but the Spirit of

God was there like a lightbulb inside this man, inviting him to see that he still had time to experience love and joy in his lifetime and that He had given him the gift of family if he would just engage with it.

That night he talked to his grandson and became a believer. As I watched, I could see that same thread on him as those on the other human holograms, and it was linked right back into the Father's heart. All that this man had become on his own—by using the glory God gave him when He created him in His own image—was now dwarfed in comparison to the fully reintegrated life of love and connection I was seeing now in the man.

I could see the seed of his original form and design that had been ignited to life, and I was so happy for God. I was so happy for this man. I was so happy that something so simple was the catalyst for redemption. I got to meet up with him later on, and what I saw in this heavenly vision was exactly what had happened.

HATRED OF THE FALL

I was back with the angel, looking at the Trinity laughing, and I was in holy wonder over all that they were crafting. But after seeing these two people, I was so angry at sin and the fall and at Satan. We were meant to be glorious, and when I thought back to my earthly life compared to what I was seeing here, I was resentful.

"Have you ever read a book and hated parts of it but loved the outcome and the ending?" the angel asked. I could think of several. "It's OK to hate parts of the story. These things were never meant to happen to people. The reason God can have so much joy in the beginning is because He is eternal. He knows what will happen from now until you are brought back into the eternal self

He created you to be." The angel walked into my line of vision, right into my gaze.

"When Jesus was on the earth, He was like you [I couldn't imagine that being true, but I got his point], except that He knew He was connected to these perceptions from the Father that started here. He began to share from this heart, soul, and mind connection over each person He came in contact with. He knew who they were, who they could be eternally. Jesus saw this reality in every interaction when He was on the earth. He weighed every conversation with His Father's perceptions.

"Look..." I was transported through time to a place I didn't recognize, but I saw Jesus there. He was in a village, in a garden that was up on a hill. The garden was behind someone's house, and it was rustic but beautiful. There was only one lantern there, but the moon was very bright that night and everything was lit well. Jesus looked over Jerusalem but also lay on the ground and cried mournfully. I knew I was looking at the night when He had already asked the Father to take the cup of suffering from Him. I had come right after this mysterious and horrible moment.

My eyes were opened to the spirit realm.

I saw all of heaven around Him in the spirit! All the angel armies were in battalions, ready to go to war, every angel ready to help Him if they could even spare Him one ounce of anguish. Then I saw the Father in heaven, looking at His Son with something in His eyes that only a Father whose son is suffering can understand. I remember visiting a friend whose son was in the hospital dying of cancer. I remember his eyes as he looked at his son. There was so much pain in them. It was like it was torture to look at his child, yet he couldn't look away. That's what the Father's eyes looked like.

Then the Father closed His eyes, and the Spirit moved from His being toward Jesus. The Spirit they shared began to pulsate with power. Jesus was being pumped full of something that He hadn't seen in fullness in His entire earthly life.

Then Jesus was back in the place before the beginning, looking at each of us, looking at each human hologram and laughing and marveling at what the Godhead had created together.

That place of joy was back in His heart, and the anxiety of having to suffer the next day was gone as He saw us, and He had joy again because He knew we—you and I—were worth it.

He looked at you, and in the garden He smiled.

On the hardest, most miserable day of His life, you made Him smile. "Fixing our eyes on Jesus, the pioneer and perfecter of faith. For the joy set before him he endured the cross, scorning its shame, and sat down at the right hand of the throne of God" (Heb. 12:2, NIV).

You Were the Joy Set Before Him

When we think of this sentiment, it's not just poetic. Jesus literally knew you, saw you, and wanted you. He was in the garden in stress, to the point of bleeding, and then He saw you—and that moment changed His frame of mind. He couldn't wait to be with you. The memory of you and what you were supposed to be was not enough just for Him to endure the cross; it was enough for Him to also cross over to get the keys to the kingdom back.

That memory of you filled Him with so much joy that He was filled with excitement about sharing everything with you again.

Of course, He also saw His role and title reinstated after the cross, but you have to realize that He already had those before He came to earth as a man. He didn't need to do anything to get that back. He came to the earth for something far more significant.

Positional, eternal authority wasn't the purpose of the cross.

You were His purpose. He saw what He and the rest of the Trinity had designed from the beginning. It was in their master plan. Paul wrote of it to the Ephesians:

> But God still loved us with such great love. He is so rich in compassion and mercy. Even when we were dead and doomed in our many sins, he united us into the very life of Christ and saved us by his wonderful grace! He raised us up with Christ the exalted One, and we ascended with him into the glorious perfection and authority of the heavenly realm, for we are now co-seated as one with Christ! Throughout the coming ages we will be the visible display of the infinite riches of his grace and kindness, which was showered upon us in Jesus Christ.
>
> —EPHESIANS 2:4–7

God is about to display one of the greatest presentations of His infinite riches of grace on our generation. And it's going to have a domino effect from this generation forth.

If you were a man and not Jesus, and it was you in the garden being asked to die for humanity, you would be tempted to see what humanity was not. You'd notice the moral corruption, the disobedience, the falling away, all of our failures. You might have seen humanity for all its flaws and said, "It's not worth it." You didn't create humanity, though; you didn't know what God knew and knows. You didn't see, nor have you seen, the riches of grace that God is going to pour out over the moral bankruptcy.

Jesus was eager to go to the cross from that point on *because He saw you.* He saw us. He knew this was the finish line. He knew that His suffering was the key, all the way through. He knew He could ask us to sacrifice anything and everything because He was going to set an example of it, and when we saw His example, we would have the courage to do like Him. He knew that if He could show us whom and how He loves, we would be able to have humanity as the joy set before us too and joyfully endure the cross we have to bear in our lifetime.

The angel looked at me and said, "Who is the joy set before you?" I went on a three-year journey to find the people I am called to love, to sacrifice for, to sometimes die for. It changed *everything*.

CHAPTER 5

HOW YOU HAVE FALLEN, O MORNING STAR

I DON'T KNOW EXACTLY what the coming war will look like at the end of the age, as far as the actual battles, but I know what the enemy is doing now spiritually.

The angel that was with me said, "You need to know God's enemy. We have a devil that is very jealous of you humans because you were made to be like God before time began. You were made to create and steward and enjoy. Satan's whole failure was that he thought he was responsible for the glory he was created with. He thought he could do more for the universe than God could. He had tasted God's glory and power and believed he was more worthy. When he left heaven, he really felt he could win the war against God; he didn't leave as a failure in his own mind. But as he left, he was stripped of and from that glory and power and everything the nature of God had made him."

What a slap in the face it must have been when Lucifer saw man being created. God didn't hide it from anyone. He boldly pursued His original purpose and created man, who was more like God than Lucifer would ever be and yet was created from the soil in the ground!

Lucifer was fashioned from God's own glory directly, and he was the chief architect of glory in heaven. He was the one who would be considered the artisan of artisans, with the most majestic tools and angel armies at his disposal. We were nothing compared with him. Again, we were taken from the dirt of the ground in the natural realm, a realm far lower than where Lucifer was created in the heavens.

And yet God chose the dust of the earth on purpose to be a prophetic picture for us—that we were born out of the soil of everything He created to share with us. This incredibly loving God created a whole universe around a planet, and He would have His sons and daughters born from its soil—the same soil He planted and grew His tree of life in.

In the substance of the visible earthly realm, He established us from the works of His own hands, and He placed an eternity of imagination in us all. I love the revelation in the way David says it.

> I thank you, God, for making me so mysteriously complex! Everything you do is marvelously breathtaking. It simply amazes me to think about it! How thoroughly you know me, Lord! You even formed every bone in my body when you created me in the secret place; carefully, skillfully you shaped me from nothing to something. You saw who you created me to be before I became me! Before I'd ever seen the light of day, the number of days you planned for me were already recorded in your book.
>
> Every single moment you are thinking of me! How precious and wonderful to consider that you cherish me constantly in your every thought! O God, your desires toward me are more than the grains of sand on every shore!
>
> —PSALM 139:14–18

This psalm includes David's crying out for justice against those who were warring against him (vv. 19–22). In the place of deep warfare, he knew that God alone was his salvation.

Although I am sure every angel was creatively made and given creativity—even more than man in some ways—to manifest through God, they were not created to be His sons and daughters. A CEO of a Fortune 500 company doesn't hire the best CFO to be his child; he hires him to work with him to create and keep wealth. Angels were created with a distinct purpose, the main one being to operate in the spiritual realm between heaven and earth, *not* to help command all of the earthly realm. Lucifer wanted more. And he was removed from his position as a result. Isaiah wrote, "Look how you have fallen from your heavenly place, O shining one, son of the dawn! You have been cut down to the ground, you who conquered nations" (Isa. 14:12).

Then God created man. It was always part of His intention and plan; it was in the master design, but Lucifer didn't know that. Maybe he had been part of discussions, but he didn't really know what was in the mysterious, everlasting God's mind.

God did something that was a slap in the face to Lucifer. It was the ultimate display after Lucifer had given up everything. God freely gave humanity what Lucifer tried to take in heaven. When he saw that we were freely being given what he had wanted all along—to be like God, to share His image and His sonship—Satan flipped! It was too much.

Lucifer tried to steal positional authority from God while in heaven. This was freely being given, in a greater measure, to the least of these humans he watched. He was only the creative director of God's glorious nature, but we were made to walk in God's glory *just as He does!*

When Satan deceived Adam and Eve, he probably thought it was over when they were hiding from God, but he could not see into the future. He was gloating. He felt the evil excitement of having dealt a death blow to God's plans. God had told them not to eat the fruit from the tree of the knowledge of good and evil, and they disobeyed. Satan was expecting them to be banished just as he was—they would be cast out, and then he could torment them and God all at once. He thought he had won a great victory in his battle because of our weakness, a weakness that was similar to his. Adam and Eve wanted to wield the glory of God but didn't understand that the only way it can be sustained is through connection to the Father.

The angel looked at me again and asked, "Do you want to know the biggest blow God gave Satan before the cross?" He had a twinkle in his eye when he asked the question.

"When Adam and Eve had to leave the garden, God did not do what He did to Satan and the other heavenly angels involved by removing His nature and all His glory from them. All the tormenters were watching, so happy to have corrupted God's favorite beings, but then God did something only God could do. He spoke to Adam and Eve like a father. He gave them a promise that from their very DNA, one would come who would destroy the serpent underneath his feet."

The angel walked forward with his hands clasped behind his back as he said the next thing with what seemed to be excitement and victory in his voice. "Then God did something even more awesome than promising them deliverance. He didn't remove His nature from them, nor did He remove all that He had created them for. He didn't remove their gifts, talents, affection, love, poetry, creativity—none of it. It was hardwired into them. And He didn't remove their capacity for glory. In this, He really was making a statement to all of heaven and earth, to angels and demons, that they were His children. The only thing that could remove His glory from them was if they rejected it completely in death, if they died not receiving His relationship. He gave them a lifetime to become reconnected."

I saw the third of heaven that had fallen, the beautiful fallen angels. They were furious and confused. God had pulled a trump card and hadn't judged man nor handed out the same sentence He had given the angels. He had truly made them different. This was the biggest kick to Satan's proverbial teeth that God could have given—to validate that Satan had only ever been a helper instead of a king.

I wish this were a metaphorical battle, but it's not. Satan is on a mission still to this day, and he keeps pulling out all the stops to strategically kill, steal, and destroy so that humanity will be separated from God. He has wanted to destroy us from day one.

Each person he takes down is a bullet to the heart of the Father. If you had eight kids and now you have only seven because one has died, you aren't passé about it just because you have so many left. You will mourn that loss for the rest of your life.

The Wilderness

"I want to show you one of my least favorite times in history," the angel said to me. I immediately saw what looked like a humongous screen, and on it were scenes from the life of Jesus.

As a young man, Jesus had an awareness that it was almost His time. His nearness to God, His connection to who He was, and the revelation of love that was flooding Him were about to be deployed for His earthly mission. He was fully God but not fully aware yet, and He hadn't entered into what He prayed later in the garden: His being one with God (John 17). It was already true, but He was still growing in favor with, or connection to, God and man (Luke 2:52). This growth in favor wasn't based on His actions but on learning to be one with God.

Have you ever thought about the fact that after waiting thirty years to enter into His sovereign purpose, to manifest the kingdom of God and restore it to humanity, Jesus went to fast and pray? Have you ever set aside time to really pray or fast? We all have an expectation of what God will do when we are setting ourselves apart to Him, and I am sure that's what Jesus felt when He was drawn to the desert and wilderness. He thought He was about to spend time connecting to the Father, but instead of a monastic experience, Jesus had His humanity assaulted to the point of absolute temptation because Satan was prowling around him like a lion, trying to get the victory.

Satan saw another chance to destroy the work of God. He knew that if he created division within God, he could essentially create chaos on the earth.

He wasn't stupid, so what he offered Jesus was a twisted take on what Jesus was already going to inherit from the Father. He offered Jesus a corrupted, fast-tracked version of His inheritance that the Bible says was tempting. The word *temptation* isn't a light word, and we all know what it means. This was not Jesus thinking about the tub of ice cream in the freezer He shouldn't eat; this was Jesus about to go through the hard work of redeeming humanity to their Father in heaven—whom they had all but forgotten.

He came at a time when Israel was being occupied by Rome, and there were very few true believers left. Israel was a day away from being destroyed or completely corrupted. The word of the Lord had been rare for hundreds of years. It had been a long time since God had spoken and helped Israel. It was a time of moral depravity in Rome and corruption in the leadership of Israel.

Jesus came in one of the darkest times in history for God's people. He already loved humanity with the true love of God, and He was broken over us. Because it was such an ominous time, and because Jesus was only just entering into the fullness of the revelation of who He was and what was to come, and His bond or connection with the Father, there must have been something in Satan's offer that tempted Him.

"What was the temptation," I asked the angel, "the real temptation?"

"None of us fully knows, but it had to do with trying to create division within God Himself," he said.

I have pondered this a lot. I think it was the temptation of a quick fix of deliverance for the Jewish people and being able to rule and reign over humanity immediately, bringing whatever justice He knew was right. Remember, Jesus had not been glorified yet, but He could feel the weight of God's passion for humanity and how it needed Him.

Satan was tempting Him to separate from the Father—not just from the Father's will—and lead from His own desires. I imagine Satan said something along the lines of, "Come now, I will submit and end my battle with humanity if You will only serve me instead of Elohim. Look at how they are suffering. It can *all* stop right now. You can have everything You want! We can do this now! You don't have to suffer for them, and they don't have to suffer anymore. What is Elohim even offering? He isn't going to make You like Solomon and give You a natural kingdom that is set up here and now. He wants to win the battle from the inside out, but if we change the outside, the inside will heal. Trust me." Satan likely showed Jesus this possibility from the top of the temple, thinking he was offering Him the whole world.

This is still one of the greatest battles we face: the temptation and failure to walk through the Father's process, the temptation to get an advantage and sometimes live in a lower way, or even to submit to this world and its processes. If Jesus had done this, it would have created a separation or fracture within God Himself. Satan knew the stakes in the battle that day, and I am sure he knew that if he lost there, he would lose his chance of getting any of the ultimate power God Himself could give him.

When his efforts to tempt Jesus didn't work, Satan turned his attention to the battleground of the human heart. If he couldn't have the ultimate power he wanted through God, he would try to get the power through us—he would use us so that he could have power until the end. He couldn't create or steward God's glory directly anymore, but he could use and steward God's glorious nature through us—through our talents, governments, businesses, and everything man can have dominion over on this side of eternity. He's a dictator of sorts, operating through lies, death, and destruction.

Destroy agriculture and create a suffering system? Check! Control science and technology to the point that the advancements God intended are slowed down and corrupted forms emerge? Check! Cause confusion among humanity's self-identity, creating roles of power through lesser forms of expression? Check! Tear apart the nuclear family so we won't know the good image of the Father or what marriage should really look like? Check!

In my vision Satan looked more like a crime boss than a supernatural being, enjoying the power of being on top of all that is corrupt. The power of it is a drug to his destroyed nature. This might be a simplistic way of seeing him, but it does give some reason behind the madness in our world and an understanding of why he will do anything to maintain the appearance of power, even after Jesus took any real authority back from him on the cross.

CHAPTER 6

THE COMING BATTLE

I WANT TO SHARE what I learned from these encounters about the coming attacks of the enemy and the victory we have against them, using biblical prototypes. This is not just a retelling of the encounters but a sharing of the perspective that came out of them and of their prophetic tapestry in a way that might help you.

Satan and his demons still have much they want to win. Remember that T-shirt some bikers and heavy metal wannabes wear: "Better to be a leader in hell than a servant in heaven"? That lust for authority is the downfall of those on a path headed to hell. They misunderstand real power; it comes from love first, not authority or might. The statement on that T-shirt is true in their book—they gave up their service with a goal of creating a power structure that would satisfy their demonic urges.

So many Christians are in denial about spiritual warfare, or they do not feel as if they have any responsibility in this arena, but it is very real, and we are only going to see it increase as we get closer to the return of Jesus. The enemy is not just trying to knock out churches; his ultimate goal is to possess, through humanity, the keys that Jesus took and is freely giving us—keys to banking, the environment, government, entertainment, education, justice, and ministry.

Think about what John wrote in the Book of Revelation: John saw the antichrist spirit over the world financial markets, and he saw the Antichrist oppressing us through a unified world. Without going into the details of what all that can mean, I want to simply point out that the enemy is fighting a battle and is arrogant about his ability to tempt and destroy humanity.

We know that the light of God has been steadily increasing, and we know His government is only developing further and will do so until He returns. We have extreme hope if we open our eyes to see *that* government being established and growing.

Back in my heavenly encounter, the angel with me began to describe three types of warfare that would be coming to those who are called and anointed with God's favor and appointed by God for His assignments and connection. This warfare can be broken into three biblical prototypes:

1. The attacks against dreamers like Joseph.

2. The attacks against social transformers like Esther.

3. The attacks against those who would influence and occupy government, as Daniel did.

I'm going to examine each of these biblical prototypes, but I will spend the most time on Joseph.

THE ATTACKS AGAINST THE JOSEPHS

Joseph's attack is one of the most ruthless because it comes from people you know—people who should be on your team, who should have your back, who should be working with you and not against you.

When Joseph had his dream, his brothers were confused and jealous, and they felt threatened. They didn't see themselves as great leaders appointed by God and favored for social influence and authority, and they definitely didn't want to be ruled over by their brother. They were looking for God to lead them but thought they would just live in survival mode until He did.

They didn't understand their day-by-day connection to God's eternal plan, nor did they grasp that God cared about the coming famine, Israel's future, and even other people groups such as the Egyptians. The brothers were consumed by a mediocrity and normalcy that God never intended them to have, and instead of seeing Joseph as an asset, they were threatened by the favor he seemed to have—not only with their father but in life.

Part of the attack that has come against modern Josephs is that their superior ideas of how God can manifest His kingdom seem extreme to those following Christian norms, those who claim to know what's best when it comes to God's calling and individuals' influence. So much of what Josephs perceive as reality is seen as a threat, as being too progressive, even if they have conservative moral theology. Josephs are dreamers and challengers to things that have ruled and reigned in the hearts of those around them, often for decades. They are disrupters to the current state of church and Christian affairs, and they repeatedly ask why over many status quo, comfort areas of Christianity.

Many Josephs believe God is going to change the face of Christianity in one generation. We see the greatest display of that through Martin Luther and the great Protestant reformation. There is another reformation coming, and God is commissioning people who will be more disruptive to the "religious mountain" than Uber was to the global transportation industry.

These reformers, these Josephs, have gifts for building and strategic entrepreneurial minds that are sometimes a threat to those around them who don't think great change is necessary.

Three Modes of Attack Against Josephs

We see three strategies of attack in Joseph's life.

1. The dagger—the attack from within

The attack against Josephs usually comes from within in the form of betrayal from close friends, business partners, other friendly businesses, or even ministries. It's one of the most painful attacks because it's from those who are supposed to be with you and for you. Perhaps you have experienced this attack, but if you have not, don't anticipate that this has to happen. You may never experience the pains of this experience, especially if you allow God to align you relationally and you avoid the pitfalls of Joseph's early years. God is giving the body of Christ more relational intelligence and spiritual discernment, which I think is helping us to navigate with more maturity and wisdom and less conflict avoidance.

The victory: The victory was in Joseph's long game of waiting for God to rebuild his family and life. When his brothers came to him for help, he had to keep an open heart to God's love for them and recognize why he was raised up to his destined role in the first place.

2. The sword—the attack of external jealousy

Another type of attack is from those who cannot create the change that Joseph can or who don't organically bear the authority he had, like Potiphar's wife. Her husband chose to give Joseph leadership over his life, but Potiphar's wife wanted that control. She felt entitled to it and tried to seduce Joseph so she could manipulate him and place him under her power. When he resisted, hell broke loose and he was falsely imprisoned.

So many people go through a similar attack on their life journeys. You may not be qualified positionally in the same way someone else is, but you get the opportunity, the contract, the job, and the authority God wants you to have because you have favor and the right heart. This creates insecurity, anger, and competition in the people around you. People want things all the time, and they try to get them through education, hard work, climbing social ladders, and politics. When you rise up and bypass some of that effort, they feel it shames their hard-earned progress, and sometimes it puts a target on your back.

Paul mentioned that this bypassing of the secular order of things proves we are in relationship with a living God. "He chose the lowly, the laughable in the world's eyes—nobodies—so that he would shame the somebodies. For he chose what is regarded as insignificant in order to supersede what is regarded as prominent, so that there would be no place for prideful boasting in God's presence" (1 Cor. 1:28–29).

Joseph remained in prison for another two years when the chief butler neglected to mention him to Pharaoh, but God always preserves us—even in the midst of the prisons the enemy tries to relegate us to—and turns our times of imprisonment into seasons of thriving. As a matter of fact, the prison turned out to be one of the very places God used to fine-tune Joseph's skills and talents, including his spiritual ones.

God's process for defeating the attacks on our lives is always so different from the direct road we would choose because He wants to make the most of the opposition by growing our oneness with Him in that season.

The victory: The victory only came as Joseph trusted that the environment he was currently in wasn't his end and that God would still bring him into fullness. Being imprisoned wouldn't define his success, but his time there would never be wasted.

3. The prison—the attack of being shunned

This might be the worst attack because it's when people create such a judgment against you that they shun you. It usually comes from an entire organization, with a big contract or business deal, or another ministry. Sometimes it's subtle. Joseph's character was maligned in some very strong ways, and then he was ostracized for it and banished to prison.

The victory: The victory comes from letting God build your reputation, not trying to redeem it yourself. It doesn't mean avoiding conflict, but it does mean accepting that you can't change anyone's beliefs about you—only God can. We don't have any record of Joseph trying to get out of prison, although he knew it was not supposed to be his final destination. Instead, he let God worry about the plan. He spent his time there trusting God for deliverance rather than trying to escape, and he became the second-in-command of everything in the prison—not as a guard or a prison worker but still as a prisoner. God wants us to turn our prisons into the training ground for our promotion.

Emerging Into Promise

When Joseph emerged out of the prison, the landscape of Egypt and the surrounding lands had changed. The wealth of Egypt was unrivaled at the time, but even with all of that, a natural disaster was about to occur that no money or resources, no wise man or businessman, could save them from. Only a foreign God who had an agent in their prison system could help (which makes me dream with God about who is imprisoned in the nations today).

God knew and raised up a man who had His Spirit to provide supernatural resolutions to problems that were spiritual in nature. The drought might have been a natural occurrence, but the enemy would try to use its impact to destroy Israel, among other people groups. God saw it coming and raised Joseph up as part of His solution for blessing and protecting His people.

Spiritually rooted problems exist right now all over the earth, problems that our greatest minds, our most powerful businesses, our most progressive science cannot fix. That doesn't mean there won't be intellectual answers or business strategies to open up the solutions, but they won't come from man's strength.

The power of the anointing on Joseph was not in his favor, his influence, or his gift to interpret dreams. It was in his connection to the God of heaven, who had intentions, dreams, and passions for the humanity Joseph lived among. Joseph stood as His representative between heaven and earth.

The fact that Joseph could be betrayed multiple times and imprisoned with the worst people and still believe the two fellow prisoners who wanted a dream interpreted might have had a revelation from God is astounding. Most Christians today would have given up on and judged those prisoners as unworthy, especially if they were in survival mode in their own dream life. But Joseph saw that God's holy nature was at work on everyone in the situation, not just on the Israelites, and that God even had a plan for a pagan nation that held the world's wealth.

The Attack Against the Esthers

The spiritual attack against Esther was just like the spiritual attack Elijah faced later through the possessed woman Jezebel. This spirit, or the spiritual dynamics this oppression brings, is one of the enemy's primary weapons against the people God is appointing in this generation.

Jezebel wanted to smite anyone who opposed her agenda. When we see this spirit in operation, it looks like lust, seduction, and false power. We often think this spirit that so demonized Jezebel appeared for the first time in history through her, but the spirit that was behind her was more ancient and wily. It did not begin with her. It was a spirit of death and abortion to God's purposes. Jezebel worshipped a false god that many killed their firstborn to appease. It was a spirit that sought to commit genocide against people groups and destroy the nuclear family by creating bonds through death that would ruin someone's conscience forever—all to gain power.

Scholar Jacob Hoschander wrote in *The Book of Esther in the Light of History*:

> Haman in the book of Esther is the main antagonist. His name is associated with Ahiram who the spirit of destruction was but also the name Momaes in Old Persian which meant illustrious. Haman was also a priestly title, not his actual name. In this we can see that this man had a mad quest for illustrious power religiously and would do anything to destroy those who opposed him.[1]

Whether it was because of his religious devotion to a god that wanted destruction or his own ambition, Haman operated in the same spirit against God's people that Jezebel later displayed so well. He wanted genocide for the sake of his own power.

We see this spirit operating against God's people today in government, in entertainment, in education—in all the different places where an Esther can emerge. A prophet I know once prophesied something that is so relevant here. He said that for every Esther who won't take her place, there is a Salome who is glad to go before the kings instead—with an agenda to destroy those who are precious to God.

Salome was the daughter of Herodias, the queen of Galilee, who was divorced from Herod Antipas. Herodias hated John the Baptist and plotted to kill him, so she sent her daughter to the king and manipulated his lust for Salome to get what she wanted. Both Esther's king and Salome's king gave them the same response: you can have what you want—up to half my kingdom. This prophet was making the statement that if we don't take bold risks and fight for the cause of Christ, as Esther did, the enemy has a counterfeit ready to take that position and use it to destroy the people of God.

God is anointing groups in industries, science, education, politics, and entertainment, and the enemy wants to destroy them all. The battle here is to take out what God is anointing before it can come into its full promise. The battle is also usually very public, such as with a cancel culture attack that has lots of false allegations. The enemy takes pieces of truth and tries to use them against you.

The victory: The victory comes in knowing that the enemy activates a spirit of genocide against God's anointing, His people groups, and Christians with any authority in cities, the marketplace, government, education, and industries. Our victory comes when we stand in our God-given identity and take our rightful place, even though we will face the threat of the enemy, possibly for long seasons of time. In taking our rightful place, we give God's government time to destroy the works of the Hamans and Jezebels. Taking our place manifests His plan or will and displaces their authority.

THE ATTACK AGAINST THE DANIELS

The attack against Daniel was one of spiritual manipulation. Daniel was given the spiritual seat of power in all of Babylon. His position or title literally meant "chief of all spiritual studies and practice," but most people in those days viewed someone in his position as the chief astrologer. He had studied the various religions but not practiced any. When the attack came against him in its multiple forms, it was from people who wanted to use spiritual information and positional authority against him.

Spiritual manipulation is about manipulating others with spiritual pressure, the power of their position, and spiritual words. When someone wants their will accomplished, they use this to make others do what they want them to do. This is extremely sophisticated, and it grows. It is often one of the main attacks the enemy uses against people God wants to raise up as His spiritual leaders because it is so demoralizing, pressurizing, threatening, and stressful.

The victory: Knowing this is one of the tactics of the enemy against people who have good and innocent natures is super important. Daniel stood his ground when others tried to spiritually manipulate him and gave him an ultimatum. The way to overcome spiritual manipulation is not to avoid conflict but to stand up for yourself and power through patiently.

If you stick to your principles, you may look like you are losing ground, authority, and relationship, but God will reward you and work the attack for your benefit. Those who fight a battle against spiritual manipulation by trying to fight for their reputation will often lose more of it than if they just put up boundaries and waited it out.

HEAVEN WILL FIGHT FOR YOU FAR BETTER THAN YOU CAN FIGHT FOR YOURSELF

When I ended this encounter, the angel with me showed me all the angels as if they were in one battalion or military lineup. I couldn't find their end, and the glory was so strong I was almost shaking. Even though I wasn't afraid of coming to harm, it was still intimidating. There were so many of them!

Then he said, "You know the old Pentecostal saying of greater levels, greater devils?" I smiled because I had heard this growing up in different church circles, and it had always bothered me.

"Heaven wants you to know that it should be *greater levels, greater angels.*" I knew he was saying that God and His angel armies have our back and there is nothing to fear. What can we lose when we have been given everlasting hope?

Greater levels, greater angels.

CHAPTER 7

THE GREAT PROVIDER

I WANT TO TAKE you to another facet of the vision I shared back in chapter 4. One of my favorite parts about seeing the Trinity planning each one of us was that not only were they filling us with God's nature; the Father was also planning everything we needed to develop ourselves and the world around us. He did this so we would meet Jesus ready to lay everything at His feet and have a life that's fully developed and whole, a life that blesses others and fulfills our destiny. Our lives are wired for walking in God's intentional resources and abundance, found both in our own nature and in our environment.

In the Western world, when we are preparing to have children or are expecting a child, many of us start planning and rearranging our finances and resources around the child(ren). We take on the financial responsibility of raising a child. We plan the yearly budget around what our kids will need. We dream and then plan on nurturing their talents and gifts, knowing it will cost money to give them the best programs we can provide to hone their skills. We train them to drive, either sharing the resource of a car with them or helping them buy their first vehicle from a savings account we started years earlier. We focus on what it will take to get them through college by starting a college savings account.

As parents, we can't help but leverage our personal income and net worth to give our children as great a start as we can, and often the worst part of parent guilt comes when we feel as if we haven't done enough. That is because resourcing is one of the essential means we have to develop our children. It's not always the most important, but it is very real.

Think about God in heaven as a great provider for a minute rather than as the loving yet authoritative Father we often think of Him as. See Him as one who is better than any provider the world has ever known. Think of Him before time, preplanning every resource we would need to walk out our purpose, to develop our personhood, to build our relational network. He has created us with access to so much provision and so many resources—a spiritual bank account that would blow us away if we could see what is available. I see this great storehouse of heaven over and over, and I have written about it in my book *Keys to Heaven's Economy*. I will talk more about this in a further chapter.

THE GREAT MATURING

The angel with me showed me a vision of an orchard full of trees of the same species, but they were all growing many types of fruit that were ripe and ready. "Pick something," he said with a smile.

I grabbed a beautiful, large piece of fruit that was on the lowest-hanging branch and looked at it. It reminded me of a pomegranate, but it was covered with words etched with craftsmanship into its skin. It was so gloriously artistic and looked like something out of an ancient civilization.

As I looked at the words, I realized I was reading the story of this fruit—what it was for and who it belonged to. It was a resource that was released to feed natural hunger in marginalized people groups. I knew this fruit would reveal God's love to a people who would not be able to relate to His love any other way than by being fed. Then I looked at some of the other fruit on this tree, and it was all for the same people group, and each piece was abundant with stories of its intended impact and nurturing abilities.

These stories were all about the provision and resources these people needed at different stages of their lives to become the fully formed humans the Trinity was dreaming of. It was all planted in advance, yet somehow the fruit was already mature. Just as Jesus created Adam and Eve not as children but in a mature state, somehow He planted these all as mature trees. God does this many times throughout Scripture; He brings something to maturity quickly for His purpose. Isaiah 66 is a great prophetic passage about this.

"All of these trees are already mature. What is this place?" I had to ask.

"This is the great maturing that is taking place. It has been developing since the beginning of man. The great maturing is starting with your generation."

When I came out of the vision, I was haunted by it, not fully understanding it.

Every generation of Christians wants to believe it is special, so I was having a hard time wrapping my head around the vision. Are we the most resourced of any generation? Is this a time when all the resources God has planted over past generations are coming into their mature purpose?

The Great Resourcing

The resources have been released. Now we need revelation to deploy them.

During this time of God advancing my revelation, and especially the vision of the great maturing the angel spoke of, the vision of Solomon building and Israel expanding kept reoccurring.

I kept cycling back to a huge question over and over: What is the great wealth transfer? This is a term I grew up hearing in charismatic and Pentecostal churches, and the idea comes mostly from Proverbs 13:22, "A good man leaves an inheritance to his children's children, and the wealth of the sinner is laid up for the just" (MEV). The idea is that a sinner's wealth will go to believers who will use it for kingdom purposes.

Solomon started from a place of incredible amassed wealth. David was extremely wealthy; the Bible lists his wealth (1 Chron. 18:11; 1 Chron. 22:14). Solomon led the people with a wisdom that produced wealth. Then he had his encounter with God and became the wealthiest man the world ever knew. This is an incredible theme for us. There has been so much wealth amassed in our generation. We have paper currency, gold, cryptocurrency, and stocks as well as natural, luxury, food, technology, and scientific resources we've never been able to access before.

Some prophecies about this wealth transfer go all the way back to the 1920s and speak of a time when the wealth of wicked corporations and governments will be stewarded by faithful Christians, which will bring transformation to the world. Some of these prophecies were very imbalanced and promoted poor behavior while others were simple and truthful. This prophetic theme of financial resources for Christians, though, has appeared over and over in many denominations, Christian movements and ministries, and Christian media.

When the question about the wealth transfer popped into my spirit, I began to look online for what it could mean. Scriptural research and then some natural research led me to an article written in 2015 with a lot of data about this. I felt the Holy Spirit hovering over me as I read it. He was planting insight, and I was blown away.

The article reported in 2015 that "the total wealth held by Christians stood at $107,280 billion, which account [sic] for over 55 percent of worldwide wealth."[1] To take this at plain, practical face value, we see that we have already started to operate in a measure of blessing and prosperity that would rival what hyper-prosperity gospel preachers talk about. God has put the wealth of the world (by 55 percent) into the hands of people who profess to be His children. There is an end-time setup in plain view, but most of the Christians in the world are unaware that we are set up with all the resources we need to fulfill the will of God.

For the first time in history, 50 percent of the world's wealthiest people—billionaires—claim to be Christian. This is also staggering. Something is already happening to the people who have resources that has never happened before.

Looking at this through natural eyes, we can get discouraged. There are many problems with it, the most glaringly obvious being that the wealth is not all used for the kingdom by people walking in compassion or ethics. These billionaires are not unified. Much of their spending is motivated by selfish gain and greed. But looking at this article, and remembering the angel saying that the great maturing is already happening—for the first time ever—in our generation, filled my heart with huge hope.

The Joseph Anointing That Is Coming

During this time, a strong vision came to me. I saw the Spirit moving among people all over the world in the dark of night. They were asleep in my vision, all lying in rows, all representing different nations, people groups, ages, cultures, races, and industries.

The Spirit was throwing out seeds that landed on their bodies and began to germinate within them. The seeds were the dreams of the Father in heaven. This was different from my earlier visions when I was seeing God's dreams for humanity. These seeds were the dreams of humanity in their partnership with God, like the seeds God planted in Joseph's dreams.

I knew this was a symbolic vision to show me that the Lord was planting a God dream inside His Esthers, His Davids, His Daniels, His Josephs—so many whom He sees potential within. Some of these people were not even deeply rooted in their faith yet, but He could see that they were the right soil to sow the dreams into. He knew the process and journey He would take each of them on; He knew who was qualified to carry this.

What surprised me was who the seeds landed on. If I was going to pick my A team in my natural, human disposition, I wouldn't have even noticed a lot of them. There was nothing bad about them, but they were so...normal. Would the majority of us who lead organizations have ever picked the disciples to be on our team? I never would have considered myself to be chosen to have these visions.

"You see with your eyes and what you can perceive," the Spirit said, "but I see what I created in these earthen vessels. Look again." When I looked again, I could see them in their relationship with God. I could see how the seed had matured into a mature oak tree within. They still looked very human, but the tree inside them looked like the greatest oak I could imagine.

When I looked at the ground where the roots of these oaks were invested, I realized we were standing on rich, fertile ground in a field like no other. Then we zoomed back, and I could see that the field was planted on top of God's head, and the roots were intermixed with His neuropathways!

The very thing that fed these trees, which were loaded with fruit that could change the world, was *His own* wisdom, talent, and personhood. In this vision, I could see into the mind of God and how these oak tree roots were pulsating with His powerful neurons, and it was overwhelming to think of the shared information space. (By the way, oak trees are fruit trees scientifically, as they produce fruit called acorns.)

We can understand this in a modern sense if we look at our cloud technology and how we share information when we are connected to the same network. Sometimes there are updates and advancements in our devices that make them work more efficiently. The network even connects to information we never see with our eyes or perceive as a user of the technology, but it's always advancing, always communicating. Humanity was made to be much like this with God. I believe God wants us to see ourselves in *His* headspace and know that we have access to His divinity in our plans, strategies, and purposes.

THE ANSWERS ARE RIGHT IN FRONT OF US

At one point in the vision, I saw a businesswoman in medical science and research looking for a breakthrough in her field. She wasn't thinking about the whole disease but was working on just a part of its effects. Then God sowed a dream seed, and she saw a treatment that was right in front of humanity the whole time. It was so simple and basic, something everyone could have access to because it was readily available. Scientists were already researching it, but it wasn't being applied correctly.

I heard her say, "No, this is too easy. It can't be!" But she did some preliminary tests, and lo and behold, the answers for this disease had been planted in plain sight the whole time. Last year I talked to a woman in cancer research, and she was basically telling me the same thing I saw in this spiritual vision. She said, "Some of the greatest breakthroughs are coming, and they are so simple, but we needed the field of medical science to mature and be funded like it is today to find them. The simplest cures take millions, if not billions, of dollars before they become simple."

I thought of the great maturing when she said this. I thought of diseases that have had millions and billions go into researching them and how God is going to allow a tipping point. Cancer, diabetes, AIDS, ALS—God intends to destroy every work of Satan and the fall, and many of these will have cures, some in my lifetime.

71

The angelic being that was with me in these encounters said, "Part of what will win so many to the love of God is realizing that He planted every resource humanity would need in abundance, even while world experts are saying that resources are running out or that the solutions are so complicated they can't be for everyone. In this time, the Spirit is sending us to unlock the greatest secrets, which are the most uncomplicated solutions humanity has ever known, and it will put man's wisdom and fear to shame."

Since having these visions, and even since writing this chapter, I have had many more conversations with people who are experiencing this genius from heaven in the medical fields, scientific community, and even government.

Food and health

One great recent example is a health and nutrition company led by two believers. This business is operating in some of the principles I saw, using plants that are in plain sight (and even spoken of in the Bible) to treat diseases and providing solutions for problems that seem abundantly complicated everywhere else. Their work is brilliant.

Transportation and technology

An example in the realm of transportation and technology is a company behind the new push for electric aviation transportation. The leaders shared how God is creating clean technology that no longer harms the earth and can significantly lower fuel emissions around the world—affecting everything from air quality to the materials used to build planes. It will effectively change transportation as we know it, and it's already being manufactured and purchased to serve as the primary model some airlines are using.

Education and learning

Another example is a private Christian school here in California that has developed a curriculum that is so balanced and educationally healthy that it has won awards, and it is now being used to improve many areas of California's failing educational system. During the pandemic, the founders of the school were able to distribute their curriculum through one of the largest educational platforms in South America to assist those who could not attend school, and it is estimated that over 1.2 million children started learning with their curriculum. Can you imagine seeing a generation of kids receiving a kingdom-driven education rather than a liberal, secular education?

Jesus said, "I have come to give you everything in abundance, more than you expect—life in its fullness until you overflow!" (John 10:10). When you look for it, you will find it.

In my encounter, I was looking at these Josephs and the unique central qualifier that only they were carrying—the childlike hunger and curiosity inside of them and their desire to be fed by what God is doing on the earth right now. They were searching for how His kingdom, which has only been increasing since the resurrection, is growing and moving. They were training their eyes to focus on the light in the midst of the great darkness until they could see that the light was even brighter.

This is the great delineation between those who are anointed to change culture, to bring transformation, to be seeded with God's kingdom power and those who never connect to God's heart. The former are the ones who will be deployed in finances, influence, authority, leadership, and government. So many of the best conversations are happening right now in Christianity, but what you are hungry for is what you will find to feed you.

There is such a battle in our human state for the territory of our focus. Will we focus on what God is doing and train ourselves to see it? The apostle Paul wrote:

> Finally, brothers, whatever things are true, whatever things are honest, whatever things are just, whatever things are pure, whatever things are lovely, whatever things are of good report, if there is any virtue, and if there is any praise, think on these things. Do those things which you have both learned and received, and heard and seen in me, and the God of peace will be with you.
>
> —PHILIPPIANS 4:8–9, MEV

Our alternative is to get swept away by spiritual perspective and knowledge without connecting to God's thoughts and thus become focused on what humanity is failing in, what the enemy is doing, and, even worse, how there is no hope.

When you look at a lot of the prophetic perspectives being released, reported by Christian media and even discussed from the pulpit, it's clear we spend a lot of our energy focused on what God is not doing. Those who have this Joseph seed, this appointment to bring transformation, may see these things, but what's different is that they are consumed with what God will do and who God is, not who we are not.

It's time to search deeper and connect to the author and perfector of our *faith*! When you see what God sees, you don't live with the hopelessness that everything else can bring.

CHAPTER 8

THE SEEDS OF CHANGE

I WAS AGAIN IN a vision, this time watching the Spirit sow seeds into rows of dreamers.

Before I knew why I was there, I pondered and watched, in awe of what God always intended to share with us. His intention was never for us to just play out a calling or destiny. It was for us to be live-wired to the way He is, in His own being—His energy and personality, His wisdom and compassion. I can't say this part enough: we were made in His image, and when we get plugged back in through a living relationship with Jesus, it's the most miraculously beautiful thing we have.

I was then taken back to the beginning of the process—when Jesus was being a gardener and first sowing these seeds of an anointing, which seemed as if they had the ability to release a pattern of life that both Joseph and Solomon were prototypes for. I could see the seeds in His hand, and they were brilliant! Then I could see *into* the seeds, what they were made of. I saw dreams and ideas. Some were very direct ideas that defined a noticeably clear sense of calling, but most were seeds of God's ideas that would grow and increase over time as the dreamer experienced more connectedness to God.

I loved that God's nature was the synthesis they needed to grow into maturity.

The seeds' roots caused people to desire to have a great impact. The seeds had God's DNA in them, so they were filled with wonder and possibility but were also directly programmed to grow exactly what was needed. Some people who were nurturing and growing these seeds found themselves rooted in concern about a certain social issue or people group. Others were rooted in building businesses, creative ventures, ministries, and government. Some were an intermingling of many things. To see that richly dense God seed in His root system, so full of purpose, was dazzling.

It also felt like those with the seeds could change the foundation, government, or culture of whatever they were called to, even if only incrementally. They had something inside them that wasn't calling them just to work in a certain genre but also to affect that genre.

The Spirit was seeding humanity with an expectation of anointing to bring great change. In the vision, millions of people were having dreams about their futures as they lay sleeping. Indirectly, I was seeing exactly what would play out. They would have rich, impactful lives with God, just like Joseph and Solomon had. They had dreams about influencing influencers, having authority and favor, being dressed for their occupation of leadership, and seeing changes that whole generations never fathomed could happen.

THE PEOPLE WHO WEREN'T

On the outskirts of the dreamers, though, were people who were wide awake to the world around them but not aware of Jesus, the gardener, with His seeds and seed packets. Just as those who were being seeded had a distinguishing mark, so did those who were not being seeded. They were people like Joseph's brothers, who were comfortable being "normal." They were surviving in their existence. Some were even living out of their religious principles, but they were living without connection to God. Many were positioned to spend vast amounts of time in church, following the traditions of worship. They seemed, in my estimation, to be good people, but there was one thing different about them: there was nowhere for seeds to land. There was no soil or place in them for the seeds to be sown.

I was confused, but when I looked inside of them, I realized they all had something in common—they were not dreamers. They were those who thought social justice, racial equality, agricultural transformation, medical science, city building, entertainment and arts, media, architecture, and so many other incredible subjects that were among the seed packs in God's belt were not necessarily areas they could influence. Or they even felt they were less important than religious activities.

They were limited to their own understanding of how to walk out a spiritual life on the earth. This oftentimes created confusion and dualism, even within themselves. This did not make them bad, but their religious conception limited them. Their lives were small because of their lack of connection or relationship with God. It reminded me of the parable of the ten virgins.

> When my coming draws near, heaven's kingdom realm can be compared to ten maidens who took their oil lamps and went outside to meet the bridegroom and his bride. Five of them were foolish and ill-prepared, for they took no extra oil for their lamps. Five of them were wise, for they took flasks of olive oil with their lamps. When the bridegroom didn't come when they expected, they all grew drowsy and fell asleep.
>
> Then suddenly, in the middle of the night, they were awakened by the shout "Get up! The bridegroom is here! Come out and have an encounter with him!" So all the girls got up and trimmed their lamps. But the foolish ones were running out of oil, so they said to the five wise ones, "Share your oil with us, because our lamps are going out!"

"We can't," they replied. "We don't have enough for all of us. You'll have to go and buy some for yourselves!"

While the five girls were out buying oil, the bridegroom appeared. Those who were ready and waiting were escorted inside with him and the wedding party to enjoy the feast. And then the door was locked. Later, the five foolish girls came running up to the door and pleaded, "Lord, Lord, let us come in!"

But he called back, "Go away! Do I know you? I can assure you, I don't even know you!"

That is the reason you should always stay awake and be alert, because you don't know the day or the hour when the Bridegroom will appear.

—Matthew 25:1–13

We see that five virgins had oil and five did not, and when the bridegroom came, only five were able to run to him. The rest didn't get to enter into their purpose. This is exactly what I was seeing; the ratio was even the same. I saw unbelieving believers whose greatest tragedy was that they were missing out on what God is already doing on the earth because they had no oil to see it.

But the dreamers, the ones who were connected to God's heart and purpose, were walking through some of the same seasons as others, when not much was happening yet or where transformation wasn't as evident, but they were still believing. They were still focusing on hearing God stories and seeing God's kingdom move, even if it didn't seem available in the moment. They were hungry for all God had for them in each moment, and they had faith He would do what He had planned for and through them. They were not asleep in their hearts, even while waiting for God to bring impact through them and in their families, relationships, and purposes.

While God was giving dreamers seeds, the others were unseeded, and their numbers were so great it scared me. I was checking my own heart as I saw this condition. Their lack of dreaming also caused confusion, division, jealousy, and even persecution of those who were willing to dream with God.

God's love is no different for all, but His empowerment is.

SELF-IMPRISONED CHRISTIANS

Picture a two-generation family that is wealthy from a family business the parents started. Hopefully, the parents love all their children the same. But if one child started down a path of making great mistakes, possibly even ending up in jail for a time, the parents would be forfeiting their responsibility and connection to the rest of the family if they let that child continue to work in the business. No matter how much the parents love and value him or her, the child would not be trusted. If one child had no ambition to grow and help the family business or did not share the dream, the parents probably would not create a position for that child in the business. This would be an example of the unhealthy nepotism we have seen in the past.

If, however, they had a child who was motivated to create new ways of doing business, with the legacy of the family business as the foundation, the parent-child relationship would have the added element of family purpose. Having their child's heart in the business would create a different dynamic than the parents would have had with the other two children mentioned.

This is what is happening all over Christendom.

We have the imprisoned Christians—who are stuck in the jail of their own religious limitations, bad theology, and bad choices.

We have the halfhearted Christians—who are not surrendered to Jesus as their Lord and Savior here on earth, so they still live their lives the way they want to. They include Him but do not abandon themselves to Him. They are trying to do things *for* God but aren't doing it out of relationship *to* or *with* God.

We have the surrendered Christians—those who say, "Not my

will but Your will be done." They recognize that their time on earth is about giving Jesus their lives. They know He has promised to give us all things in the eternity that is to come, so acquisition of it now is not their focus.

The love God applies to all three is the same, but the responsibility is very different, so the empowerment, resources, and blessings don't flow the same. We are not dealing with a King who favors one over another by His own whims. The power of His favor is in our hands and hearts; He is ready to give it.

The Resources to Carry Out the Purpose

I have been walking some of these things out in my life. Sometimes the Old Testament prophets' lives and what they were doing—or what was happening to them—were a message for Israel. The events of their very lives would be a prophetic journey that Israel could interpret and see what God was saying. This has happened with me in quite a few ways.

When we first moved to Los Angeles, it was during a time of recession in America. There was also an entertainment strike, so LA was hit with a double recession. We weren't sent out with support from a network, and most of our ministry partners stopped giving when we moved because they didn't feel connected to our sense of calling to California. Some even said they didn't believe God could do anything good in LA.

It sounds ridiculous now, but many of the ministries we were involved with had already handed LA over to hell in their hearts. So when we told them God was sending us, they all but renounced us. It was very strange, and I am glad that over time God restored and realigned some of these cherished relationships.

When we were moving to LA, I heard Jesus say, "I am homeless in many places, and I am homeless in Hollywood." Shortly after that, I saw a homeless man on the streets of Hollywood who looked like the images we see of Jesus, and I felt burdened. I knew some of the ministries and churches in Hollywood were definitely wonderful, but there just weren't that many of them when compared with the population. As a matter of fact, we were told by a church research group at that time that to reach the needs of those living in Los Angeles, more than two thousand *more* churches needed to be planted. It was a wasteland. The churches that were good were awesome, but there was room for so many more.

I felt we weren't supposed to just start having gatherings but that we needed to launch a church. This was counterintuitive when we didn't have a sending group, the nation was in recession, and just the year before we arrived, church statistic groups reported that Los Angeles was the hardest city in America to build a church in. But off we went with dreams in our hearts.

I met with a real estate agent to help us find a home to rent. The prices were beyond what we could have imagined after living in the Midwest, where I remember renting a room at age nineteen for $250 a month—and I thought that was almost too much! Now I was in LA, where we could not find a house for four people to share for less than $3,000 a month.

Before coming to the city, I had two days to look at the houses the real estate agent had lined up for us to view. The houses happened to be everywhere but where I wanted to live. I was praying on the morning of the house tour, and I heard the Holy Spirit say, "Solomon built a temple with great resources because he knew I was worthy of it. If you knew Me this way, you wouldn't be looking for a church property and houses the way you are looking."

I was immediately convicted but also clueless. "What can I do, God?" I thought. I was scheduled to leave in two hours. Then I applied a spiritual process to the house search. I felt I should be proactive and look myself. I said, "God, I am going to look up rental listings in areas I feel pulled to live in, and I am going to try and look with Your eyes."

I didn't know where to start. I knew about one rental website that listed the majority of rentals in LA, and it just felt right to look there. I put in what I thought were the right criteria, and instead of looking for a church property and a house, I looked for a house that also had a work and meeting space. If Jesus was homeless in Hollywood, I was going to find a holistic space where we could birth a house for Him to live in. I left the price field blank, and the houses that came up started at $11,000 and ranged up to $125,000 a month, and this was in 2007! Most of the houses I was looking at weren't even that nice. Some of the nicest houses in the Midwest cost less to lease per month than the cheapest one listed in LA, and, surprisingly, even most of these were in desperate need of remodeling and care.

I looked through the typical listings that showed the front of the houses until I just got afraid to look any further and stopped. I opened my bank account page and saw that I only had $7,000 in my account. I had lost everything in the recession. I had good credit, but it wouldn't carry over with a new organization, and it looked like I was just a start-up. I knew I would never be able to afford something from the listings I was looking at.

I texted my assistant to ask what we had in the ministry account— so I could propose a weekly rental space to the board to start our meeting together. Even renting something once a week from the listings was $3,000 or more a month. I was experiencing a rude awakening. After all monies were designated for the next few months, our savings had dropped to only about $15,000 total in our account, and we needed an office and weekly space and a place to live. We knew offerings wouldn't carry us for a while, and our partnership was dead. I was out of my league.

I thought back to a family that had graciously offered our

ministry a $9 million multiuse, luxury property with a $1-million-a-year budget—if we would just move to the Midwest. I clearly knew it wasn't God for us to move, so we said no, but now here I was in LA with nothing, yet I felt God ask me to do even more than partner with Him. "Oh, how I wish that financial situation was available for this," I was thinking.

Then I felt the Holy Spirit pulling me back to the computer screen, and I heard Him say, "Don't be intimidated or limited by what you have; be aware of the resources we have together." A statement popped into my spirit: "The provision you need comes with the destiny I give you. Don't be afraid."

In my spirit, I again saw the people who had been seeded with God's dream—those who were called to be oaks of righteousness, those who were dreaming with God. I began to pray for them, and as an act of intercession—not only for what I was called to but for all of them—I came out of my hesitation and said, "I will obey!"

God was giving me a hope that was unfounded, far outside our current financial status. I looked through the listings again, and one all but jumped off the screen into my heart. "This is our home for a year!" I said out loud. But it didn't make sense because it was a $12,000 house reduced to $9,000 a month, and it also required a first and last month payment *and* a deposit *and* proof of funds to even be considered. I did the math in my head for all the costs and additions they had on the listing and thought, "I don't have $33,000!"

I was about to click close the listing, but the Holy Spirit said, "The only way you will be able to live in LA is if you follow Me." So I called the listing agent, Jamie, and he answered on the first ring. I told him we were moving to LA and needed the house, and he asked if I had proof of funds and what kind of job I had. I told him, "I don't have proof of funds and we are starting over in our ministry, but I promise we have integrity. We will take care of this house as if it's our own, and we have amazing references."

He paused and said, "I really shouldn't show you the house, but I am showing it to a doctor today. If you want to come right after him, I will already be there and can walk you through since it's vacant."

I called my real estate agent, an awesome Christian lady, and said, "I have a house for us to look at up in Studio City, Hollywood area."

She said, "We will never make our other appointments because of traffic. You can't afford that house. Let's just stick to the plan. You have two days, then you have to go back home, and you are moving in less than a month!" She didn't want the bunny trail.

I said, "I am going with or without you. I am so sorry that you did this work for me and that it looks like I am flaking out, but I have to walk this out." She decided to come with me to see this other house.

When I arrived with a member of our team and we got out of the car, I felt like I was on *Extreme Makeover: Home Edition* when they shout, "Welcome home, Bolz family! Welcome home!" It was exactly where I wanted to live geographically. It felt like my style of home, and it also felt spiritually significant, but I laughed to myself at the $33,000 looming over my head.

As I was walking up to the door, my assistant texted me.

> Hey, remember that South Korean church we went to? They want to send us an offering for our LA church plant and for you personally. They are wiring it tonight. They said it was $7,500 and sent Jeremiah 33:3 as a prophetic scripture.

I knew Jeremiah 33 well. "Call to Me, and I will answer you, and show you great and mighty things which you do not know" (Jer. 33:3, MEV). What was amazing, though, was the amount we needed for this house and the Scripture reference at the same time—33!

I thought to myself with a laugh, "Well, it's not even close to what we need, but it's a miracle token with a miracle Scripture reference! No one has sent us any large gifts since we started on our LA purpose."

The door was open and we walked in. I yelled to the real estate agent, laughing, "Jamie, take your sign down. We are moving in!"

Jamie, an older man, was in the backyard and laughed back. "Well now, wait a minute. You haven't even seen it."

"It's perfect! How can I talk to the owner? I need to work out a deal with him."

"Um, oh, you can't talk to the owner," Jamie said. "He's a celebrity and doesn't do his own real estate management. Also, the couple who just left are filling out an application. It's a doctor and a lawyer, and they have the money to prepay a whole year."

"They are prepaying $9,000 a month?" I said out loud, just kind of marveling at what they were offering.

"Oh, the house is only $7,500 a month; we reduced it again," Jamie said. Something inside of me hit hard because that was the amount the South Koreans had committed to us. The verse they sent, Jeremiah 33:3, was shouting God's favor in my face. This was our house. As Jamie walked us through, I could see the walkout basement being our offices, the middle floor—which was wide open—being our meeting space, and the upstairs being our living area. This old seventy-five-hundred-square-foot Spanish-style mansion hadn't been updated since the 1980s, but it was charming.

"Do you know about this house?" Jamie said, as if I knew any history at all about where I was. "This is Bennett Drive, and this is the historic Bennett House. Dr. Bennett, who built it, made history in Hollywood. He came into the entertainment industry and moved into these hills. He did think tank gatherings for lawyers, doctors, and investors on how to make money through entertainment, and how to provide quality movies and television that could change the world." Jamie's parents had known and grown up with the Bennetts' children, so this was only his word on the story, but it made so much sense.

Making History in Historic Buildings

A few years earlier, a prophetic man who didn't know we were going to LA said, "I see you making history in historic buildings in Hollywood and the surrounding area."

As we walked through, I was thinking about how Solomon apprehended the resources of countries around him to shape the kingdom of God's people. I felt so strongly that this resource—this house—had been set apart for God for such a time as this. Here we were at the Bennett House, and I knew I needed to make my appeal.

Right as I was about to talk price and business with Jamie, my assistant texted again.

> The South Korean pastor interpreting for the church that wants to give you money tonight made a mistake. It is not $7,500 once but $7,500 a month for six months.

I was in awe. My faith aligned with God's vision. Provision was unlocked and was exactly what we needed.

"Jamie, I need you to call the owner," I said. "I need to talk to him."

"I can call him," he replied. "You can't talk to him, but I will for you. I don't know why, but I am hoping this works out for you. I would like to work with you."

While he called, I looked up Psalm 75 since the rent was $7,500 a month. "We give thanks to You, O God; we give thanks, and Your name is near; Your wondrous works declare it" (Ps. 75:1, MEV). I knew His wondrous works were proving how near He really was.

When Jamie got the owner on the line, I asked if we could rent the house and if he would waive the deposit requirement of the first and last months' rent. I also asked if we could occupy it sooner than it was listed as being available. I told him we were being sent to LA by God and that we were going to work with creative people and entertainers, helping them to develop who they are. I told him we hated poverty and wanted to work with the homeless, foster care groups, and groups against human trafficking. I said we needed his house to be the incubator for it.

He said we could have it for one year, and he was excited it was going to a group of people with so much purpose. He was from a different faith, but his mother, a Baptist minister, had been praying for him, and he knew that using his resources for God was a direct result of her prayers. We were an answer to prayer, even if they had not been his prayers.

We did not even send in the full application; we just signed the contract the next day. As we walked out, my assistant texted again and said,

> The South Korean pastor said he misunderstood again and that the church actually wanted to give us a onetime gift.

I got scared at first because it took a few minutes for the follow-up text to come through. I thought, "Oh no, was I being arrogant? Was this God's will?" I almost talked myself out of it.

Then the final text came through.

> They are giving us $75,000 tonight.

I was blown away.

As a side story, a film company used the house for a project later on and paid the equivalent of five months' rent. Remember the owner of the house, who wasn't even a believer? He said, "I am not touching God's money; that's for you!" So we used it to pay the remaining rent and lived there for eighteen months.

God provides space and resources for everything you are called to.

One thing that comes with being seeded by Jesus is that we

must trust God's provisional nature. Everything God is planting takes resources to come into fullness, and He provides them.

The presence of the Lord came to me in this time and said, "Make a list of everything I have called you to, and then write down your best guess of what it will cost—the real estate you need, the human resources it will take, every type of resource that will be needed to bring it to being."

I wrote for a few hours. The dream was big, but imagining the resources needed seemed complicated. It felt overwhelming. I stopped a few times and thought, "Do I have pride? Do I really believe in this dream and understand the resources it will take to bring this kind of change and impact?"

Right then, one of my favorite prophetic people, whom I hadn't talked to in over a year, texted me Ephesians 3:20: "Never doubt God's mighty power to work in you and accomplish all this. He will achieve infinitely more than your greatest request, your most unbelievable dream, and exceed your wildest imagination! He will outdo them all, for his miraculous power constantly energizes you." And he left a note:

> God is saying whatever you're thinking about is too small and that you need to sit with Him and dream bigger because you need greater resources to fulfill His dreams in your lifetime than you can hope for or imagine, so think bigger!

I was stunned. I heard the Lord say, "Now look at the dreams again, now that you know it will take more than you feel you can produce to make them happen. Look at how big they are, surrender your unbelief, and dream bigger with Me."

I did just that, and it was freeing and scary and awesome. It felt like what I imagine the Israelites felt when they were being delivered the vision of the promised land, a land that was flowing with milk and honey and all the resources to build their country, cities, and families; a place for God to really dwell with them.

Ephesians 3:20 and the theme of imagining or dreaming with God is going to be one of the markers of the upcoming move of God. It is going to be essential that we can get out of our way of thinking and get renewed with His vision, His awareness, and His dreams over the world that He so loves.

CHAPTER 9

THE BRILLIANCE
OF MANKIND

I N THE VISION of the Trinity working on mankind before time began, which I shared in chapter 4, I saw something spectacular. Inside of every cell of humanity, God created space that He could overlap within Himself. There were three dominant spaces I could see the most interaction in:

1. The mind

2. The heart

3. The inner space or spirit around the stomach

THE SHARED SPACE BETWEEN GOD AND MAN

I saw the Father holding four young men, and He said, "Look! Even before its time!" And He lit the God network up within them in an extravagant way. Then I could see the Spirit hovering over them, and what I saw in their spirits looked like the northern lights. "To these ones we will give our divine intelligence; they will deliver Israel in a time when nothing else but this and their faithfulness will work." The Trinity was smiling over this decision. I realized I was looking at Daniel, Shadrach, Meshach, and Abednego.

"As for these four youths, God gave them knowledge and skill in every branch of learning and wisdom. And Daniel had understanding in all kinds of visions and dreams" (Dan. 1:17, MEV). In Daniel's generation, Israel was very oppressed, and the people in exile in Babylon no longer had anything of their own. Their identity was all but stripped from them. Even the four men's names were changed (Dan. 1:6–7).

Then God imbued Daniel and the three others with His mind and perceptions to show His people that He loved them, even in their rebellion. He raised the men up and placed them in unusual and unique positions for Israelites to be in, and through their choices, Israel was saved and ultimately redeemed. I could see the Godhead loving these four men and admiring the craftsmanship of what they had created and were still creating.

"These look so much like the ones who will be alive when we return for humanity in the end!" Jesus said.

"Yes, but they will stand as a beacon for what is available to those who come after You," said the Father, "deliverers who share our mind, our perceptions, and our heart again." He rubbed one gently within His large fingers.

I watched for what seemed to be hours. The Godhead pulled away from the first batch of humans they had been working on, people who would come before the cross, and started a new one. They looked the same in almost every way, except one thing was definitely different: they were now working on those who would be born after the resurrection of Christ. The capacity of the humans who would be on the earth changed; it seemed as if the Holy Spirit was a divine programmer, and the vessels became brighter. They had been predestined to be on earth after the resurrection, which gave them a different grace.

The angel who had been the narrator of these experiences was back and standing next to me. He said, "You are the habitation of the presence of our holy God! It changes you from the inside out, daily, and gives you an opportunity to partner with His brilliance anytime."

I knew this was absolute truth, but it didn't feel like practical truth to me. I have had moments in my life when God made all the difference, but what I was seeing here was an interweaving of God's incredible nature and abilities, His wisdom and perceptions, within us when we embrace Jesus. The change was night and day, and yet the actual process of it didn't often seem to happen the way I was seeing it here.

THE RECIPE

"You have access, but you have to grant His nature access by listening," the angel said. I immediately knew that was the recipe: to read the Word, pray, listen to the Holy Spirit, and then obey. That has always been the truth outlined in Scripture, but I didn't fully realize how important it was.

"Most Christians don't even believe they can hear God," I said.

"But most people are hoping to hear God," he responded, smiling. I don't think I took him very seriously when he said it. I had limited my statement to Christians whereas he had expanded it to everyone. Some time went by, and he spoke again.

"You are all hardwired to hear His voice. It's in your instincts; it's in your nature; it's in your mind; it's in your heart; it's in your spirit; it's in your senses; it's in your emotions. The problem is that most of you, even the ones who feel mature, don't believe it. When amazing things happen in your family, career, or hobby, you think you were the originator of it. Think back to the decisions that led you to that awesome moment, to that breakthrough. There you will find God!"

I was then transported to an important moment in my life, and the memory came alive.

I saw when Cherie, my now wife, moved to Los Angeles. Her best friend was living in a rented room with my best friends. Cherie ended up staying with them, and my friend Jona called me and said, "Hey, that girl from Vegas, Cherie, is staying with us for a while."

To which I said, "I'll be right over. I want to come say hi."

Jona asked, "Why? She lives here now, and she just got here. You don't have to come right away." But I wanted to come right away because I liked Cherie, and I felt a magnetic pull toward her. We began dating the next week.

When I looked back with the angel, I realized the circumstances God orchestrated to get Cherie's best friend to LA. Then He made it a safe place for Cherie to come to, and with the following of God, she did get here. Then she ended up moving in with my best friends right away, who made me aware that she was in LA almost immediately. Then I was filled with my own radical, magnetic desire to be close to her, which was like no other dating feeling I had ever had.

There were so many God moments in this story, but when I shared it with a friend just a week before this encounter, I made it sound so natural, so common. I had almost erased out God and all He had done in leading us to each other. I had become the hero of the story, not God.

I realized how infrequently I acknowledge my own spiritual and prophetic journey, and I was convicted over leaving God out. Not only was I not giving Him the credit or glory He deserved, but I also wasn't learning, through my own story, how He was leading me and speaking on so many levels. I could not repeat this success without Him because it came through His ingenuity and creativity at work gently within me. I now recognized how God was doing so much to help me to realize and make this choice. It was His glory, not mine.

The angel then began to take me through my life journey and show me the intricate, interwoven times—when God showed up and gave me His opportunities—that I had not acknowledged yet. I was in awe. I learned so much about how to see the many ways God prepares my heart, gives me opportunities to partner with Him, points out areas that are holding me back, helps me to repent of sin, and ultimately leads me. It was astonishing.

Everything changed when the angel showed me this. I was already hearing God's voice in some measure, and I understood the gifts of the Holy Spirit, but this wasn't just about gifts; this was my nature, which was wired to know Him and share my life and process with Him.

HUMAN NEUROLOGY MIMICS OUR SPIRITUAL NEUROLOGY

Neurologists have organized our brain function into many parts of our body, but we have neurons that interact with the brain *en masse* in three main parts.

The brain has over one billion neurons and is the seat of our thinking power.

The gut has between four hundred million and five hundred million neurons.

The heart has over forty thousand neurons.

Sometimes you can feel your thoughts in your heart or body because your emotions can rest in places other than just the brain. At other times you get a gut check about a decision you are making; it feels like your thinking power is even more in your stomach. These are all very real feelings that line up with how you were made.

As I was looking at the pre-created versions of us in God's

imagination, I saw a complex root system—like the systems in our brain—going throughout our whole being, but it was our spirit's system. Our physical brain functions are like a token of the spiritual functions in our inner being. When I looked within, our insides were pulsating with light. It was one of the most fascinating things I have ever witnessed.

"This is your God wiring," the angel said. "It is the master plan of God. There is nothing like it in all creation." I could see waves of blue light coming from God's thoughts, His dreams and imagination pulsating through the human beings all around me. They lit up with each feeling of bliss, brilliant intelligence, heroic character—I was in awe.

I am not trying to define a spiritual reality here; it's just how I saw it, but I saw God's Spirit overlapping a believer's spirit and intertwine, like a root system, with theirs feeding off of His. Light was firing off between God and humanity like neurons in the mind, heart, and stomach—bright as a Christmas tree.

His light pulsed through all the beings He was creating like blood pulses through a heart. His light filled them like a moving river of His nature. This is how we were made to be. Our God wiring creates connection to His very inner life that brings about all the greatness within us and through us. This is what He created us for. This is what being His living ark and temple was supposed to look like.

Then I saw it again in a slightly different way. Like our brain, our spirit is also wired with our spiritual neural network, but it is constantly being updated with God's Spirit, not just our own thoughts. When we are walking in relationship with Jesus, we actually hear His perceptions and thoughts. We have the opportunity to discern or have instinct and intuition about His will, mind, heart, and emotions.

God always intended to share His perceptions and intelligence with us. Anyone who works on anything huge (planting churches, solving world issues, creating new technologies, working within the health industry, planning education, parenting or being a spouse) knows that you will reach not only your own limits, but also some of the limits of those in that field. God never tried to create us with a limited capacity; He formed us with a need for connection to Him and His thoughts so that by joining with Him, we would be limitless.

When we look at temple worship in the Old Testament and how it was done, we see it was not as important as the presence of God the temple held. I think specifically about the ark of the covenant—the box that somehow held the presence of God. God showed the Israelites what carrying His presence could do for them. It brought them victories in battle, financial prosperity, agricultural growth, safety and security, and it proved to the world around them that they were not alone. They were able to defeat larger armies because their God dwelled with them. That time in biblical history was supposed to be a prophetic picture for us of what housing the presence of God would do in our lives today.

His presence within us is supposed to give us His nature, not just the attributes of empowered wisdom or character or the fruit of the Spirit. It feels like a lot of Christians who pursue God religiously are trying to attain virtues and character as proof that they are walking with Him. They form their spiritual opinions around the knowledge they have in their worship and biblical theology. They miss the boat, so to speak.

His wonderful wisdom and fruit and character do build in us, and they can be proof that His love dwells in us, but on top of those the living God who died for all of humanity lives *in* us. This changes our options. His nature and living light empower our personal transformation and the transformation of the world around us.

To Picture Us as Living Arks

The angel spoke to me again: "Picture it less in a medical way and more in a relational way. In the Old Testament times, over and over, people were intimidated by the people of God because they had the ark of the covenant of God that didn't just represent God's tablets in a wooden structure. No one would be afraid of a legally binding document in a box, but *this box* held His presence. He was literally hovering over His covenant to His people. If they followed Him and where it went, they could never fail. There was nothing like it. No one on earth had ever heard of a God who loved His people so much. He was present with them." The angel walked over to the edge of where we were. I hadn't noticed the edge before this moment, but it felt very important.

"What is that edge, and what is over the edge?" I asked.

"This is where human history begins," he replied. Then he went back to his message to me. "So much of Christianity has been like an ark holding legal documents, and not many outsiders are really affected by it because you haven't let God inhabit the space, so it becomes a mere box, not a living representation of God. His purpose without His presence will lead you to complicated defeats that will confuse you and take away the majesty of His nature being displayed to the world around you."

In between us, a scripture appeared in the air, hovering with majestic light. "Don't you know that you yourselves are God's temple and that God's Spirit dwells in your midst? If anyone destroys God's temple, God will destroy that person; for God's temple is sacred, and you together are that temple" (1 Cor. 3:16–17, NIV).

"What happened at Pentecost to Jesus' believers?" the angel asked me.

"They were filled with God's Spirit," I said, confident in what I had always been taught.

"Yes, *and more.*" His eyes glimmered with revelation and supernatural intelligence. "They were plugged back in fully to God, the way He intended. Their very frames, just like Adam's and Eve's, were once more flowing with His very nature, capable of anything! They had become His *living arks,* the representation of His presence on the earth. They weren't just being touched by His Spirit; they were re-created as *dwelling places of His being.*

"Jesus promised them it would happen, but they were still looking at the Spirit of God as some kind of supernatural tool kit or empowerment gift to help them start a new country or manifest a greater version of Solomon's kingdom. They thought they were going to start some new form of Judaism and take over all other religions." The angel walked right over to me and smiled his big smile, though I could barely see it because his form was so blurry. I wished I could see better here.

"God had much, much more intended, and He wasn't giving gifts that would make His people superhuman. He was giving His nature to show how whole one human could be when in right alignment and in love with their God, and how much the world would change because of that relationship. After all, Jesus demonstrated only what was available before the resurrection." He breathed in deeply as if inhaling a substance, and I realized that a fragrance filled the atmosphere. It took a second for my human senses to recognize it.

"What is that?" It was as if I was in a spa, a ripe orchard, and a vineyard all at once, like I was smelling the best essential oils I had ever smelled.

"That fragrance is coming from the mature field I showed you, the field of the great maturing that is happening right now." Although most of what he was showing me was symbolic, relating to moments of the past and even before time, I knew that at this point he was talking about the times you and I live in.

"It's not just resources that are being released; it's also the fruit of oneness with God. That fragrance that is so intoxicating is proof that what God intended for the earth is ripe. He has planned this maturing for this generation of people, both young and old. This maturing is the fragrance of a move of His Spirit that is coming. It will change and reform the practice of Christianity all over the earth."

For what felt like hours, I had a deep time of just inhaling, being, and knowing the presence of God.

CHAPTER 10

ACCESS GRANTED

ALMOST AS SOON as the vision ended, I was watching again, seeing the atmosphere close to earth from an astronaut's view up in the heavens. There were a billion little points of light below, and I could look at one, zoom in on it, and see a person. The person looked like the ark of the covenant 2.0—the individual held the *full* glory of God, and yet this was a human.

I looked up and saw that God couldn't even fit in the space He had created in time and space. His glory was too vast to fit into the universe, but somehow He had wired humanity itself to contain His being and nature. It was overwhelming, to say the least.

One point of light I zoomed in on was glorious. This person I was seeing was a woman in Australia. She had medium-length wavy brown hair, and she was working in an entrepreneurial business. The business hadn't taken off yet. It somehow combined food and technology, and she and her company were having a hard time breaking through in the industry. What she was currently seeing was discouraging; her company was running out of budget, and they had some client or investor withdraw their orders. It felt as if they were close to the end.

Then the angel of the Lord put his hand on my shoulder, and it felt like I was instantly hooked up to a huge amount of voltage, and I looked again. I saw when her idea first came to her, and it had come straight from the presence of God—in the same way the presence would make way for the Israelites. They would carry the ark from one place to another, having no doubt in God because it was undeniable what His presence over the ark did for them.

The woman was carrying this piece of God's perception and idea over food and technology, and when I looked deeper, I could see the idea was like a seed inside her. This seed held the concept of the merging of the food and tech industries in a certain way, but it also held something else. Deeper within that seed was compassion and a movement and funding for an at-risk people group. In her business idea, one that had been birthed from her connection to God, was a seed for one of God's greatest moves, but it was also being contested and warred against by the enemy.

"If she could only be present to the fact that this wasn't just a good idea; it was God's very idea. She could see what He can turn it into!" I said out loud.

Then she went to some sort of small group gathering she was involved with and asked for prayer. When the other believers prayed for her, I saw that seed open up and sprout. It started taking root and pushing forward. She was filled with something that was no longer her ability or strength but God's divine energy.

"Whoa!" I said loudly.

"When you partner with God," the angel said, "His own zeal fills you and will accomplish His purpose. You may have dark days, but what is beautiful is how this woman reconnected in one second not only to encouragement, but to the next level of growth. She is seeded with something that is so unique it might just change the condition for a whole people group. But it will also disrupt a negative aspect of the food industry because she carries something that is a simple solution to some big problems. How could He not allow it to prosper?"

The Process

"Then why is it so hard?" I asked.

"Because He is navigating her through a process that no man can endure for her. It's designed to get her to a destination that no other company has reached. Even the companies, industries, and countries that are making huge progress and leaps forward are still not on God's timing or speed, no matter how fast they look. This seed will only grow as she obeys His heart through this supernatural process that requires all of her faith. Faith isn't just a bonus gift; it's the central gift that grounds you in the fact that the living God is with you, not somewhere else, and that He will accomplish what He has for you.

"The process is different because the destination is unheard of or unknown, and it has to be if we are going to see the full return for the price Jesus paid on the cross to restore everything. *You can't expect a God result without a God process.*"

I started to think about the term "the great maturing" that the angel had talked to me about through these encounters. I realized that in the great maturing, so much of what God was releasing through His provision on the earth had never been done before. A whole generation of people was manifesting things that had never been seen.

As a part of Generation X, I have witnessed the coming of the microwave, color TV, virtual reality entertainment, computers as big as my desk (which couldn't do much), and a watch I can watch videos from or talk to others with. Half of the devices in my house are able to call anyone in the world, even on video. Compare that to telephones that were mounted on a wall and had to be carried around no farther than their cords. It has been a time of advancement that no other generation has experienced. The natural things speak of the formerly invisible things.

People are blinded right now, but God is about to open their eyes.

> Opposition to truth cannot be excused on the basis of ignorance, because from the creation of the world, the invisible qualities of God's nature have been made visible, such as his eternal power and transcendence. He has made his wonderful attributes easily perceived, for seeing the visible makes us understand the invisible. So then, this leaves everyone without excuse.
>
> —ROMANS 1:20

When we realize the leap forward we have taken on issues of technology, education, globalization, and human rights, we see that it's not just one signpost of the great maturing the angel showed me was coming; it's thousands of signposts in thousands of dimensions of humanity. We are on the verge of a global outpouring that is already an undercurrent in places and industries all over the world.

THE GREAT AWARENESS

One of the coming moves of God's Spirit is for the average person to have a great awareness of how much God loves humanity as they get served by technologies that didn't exist in their parents' generation or through therapy that wasn't even imagined a decade ago. People are going to start to recognize that the goodness on the earth has a source. As God serves them with it, the eyes of their hearts will be opened.

This great awareness is going to sprout among believers who already know God too, as they stop looking at the thief and his goal to kill, steal, and destroy. They are going to be so aware of what God is doing in places where Christians don't normally bring testimonies because they haven't observed His work with spiritual eyes. God is going to bring awareness of what He is doing in entire nations and industries, and it will change Christians' capacity for faith in one generation. It will multiply so quickly.

THE RESURRECTION TIMELINE

I saw the resurrection timeline again in the spirit. The resurrection looked like the starting point of a great race, and I saw Jesus the way Paul talked about Him to the Ephesians.

> I pray that you will continually experience the immeasurable greatness of God's power made available to you through faith. Then your lives will be an advertisement of this immense power as it works through you! This is the mighty power that was released when God raised Christ from the dead and exalted him to the place of highest honor and supreme authority in the heavenly realm! And now he is exalted as first above every ruler, authority, government, and realm of power in existence! He is gloriously enthroned over every name that is ever praised, not only in this age, but in the age that is coming!
>
> —EPHESIANS 1:19–22

Then I heard Colossians in my spirit.

> He is the divine portrait, the true likeness of the invisible God, and the firstborn heir of all creation. For in him was created the universe of things, both in the heavenly realm and on the earth, all that is seen and all that is unseen. Every seat of power, realm of government, principality, and authority—it all exists through him and for his purpose! He existed before anything was made, and now everything finds completion in him.
>
> —COLOSSIANS 1:15–17

This is how we were made to carry Him within—His victory as the supreme authority over all things in this age and the age to come. We are created in Him and wired with Him, and now we live through Him.

THE HOLY SPIRIT IS OUR ACCESS

The angel said, "The Holy Spirit wants to show you something that not many believers right now are consciously looking for but everyone needs."

Suddenly someone was in front of me. No, it was a wind! No, it was sound vibrating. No, it was color. It was a person, but He was shifting in and out of forms, and some of these forms I recognized while some I did not.

It was the Holy Spirit. The Spirit began to show me all at once the many dimensions of who He is through a creative expression of all the ways I could relate to Him. A lion, a lamb, a color, the light of the world, eyes that see in every direction, a wheel within a wheel, the King of kings, a Father who loves me, a vine that we are grafted into. Of all the things I have ever seen, this was one of my favorites.

The closer we get to the last days, the more access we will have to know God. Through the many ways He reveals Himself, He is going to unveil some of the most anointed teaching to date on His nature and who He is. We have gone through a few decades of personal identity teaching in the church, but what happens when God brings His clear truth about His own nature and identity? This will happen in every kind of Christian church on the earth. The Spirit is imparting an excitement to know God in the way He wants to be known.

The Bible reveals so many of the characteristics of who God is. When we share with someone who we are and what defines us, it helps them relate to us, champion us, connect to us, have compassion for our journey, have empathy for our choices, and connect to things through us that wouldn't be available if we were not sharing relationships.

An example is my role as a father to my daughters. Just by having me as their father, they have my resources to help build their lives, both now and with whatever I leave them. They have a measure of my time no one else in the world has. They have a focus of my heart when it's time to celebrate their accomplishments or problem solve their issues of growth. They have my empathy and compassion to provide strength during hard times. Just that one role of father gives them so many access points to my heart and relationship.

God created many access points in how He revealed and reveals Himself to man, and it's our job to discover these individualities and learn how to benefit and relate to Him in these ways. God is a father and healer; He is justice; He is breakthrough; He is all-powerful; He is so many things to us! It's why I based my show on TBN, *Discovering God*, on getting to know these very natures of God— so we can have the fullest access to Him on this side of eternity.

The Holy Spirit's job is to give us access to everything we need in the Trinity. He is between us and God and is only limited by our access card, which is our faith regarding how much we can relate to God in these various roles He plays as a loving Creator.

Our greatest warfare is in seeing God in His three main identities:

1. The Father

2. The Bridegroom or our counterpart

3. The judge

ACCESSING GOD UNTO TRANSFORMATION

Then the Spirit of God touched my mind, and I saw a vision within this vision.

I felt like there were diagrams, schematics, plans, architecture, formulas, and scientific proofs hovering in the air everywhere around me. I was floating in an ocean of brilliance, and what I was seeing could transform the way we eat or the way we sleep. I saw inventions that could add days to our lives, and I saw schematics for new vehicles and devices that would make our version of augmented reality seem boring. I felt like I was swimming but being moved by a gravitational system that seemed to pull me deeper.

Then I saw not just the plans and schematics. I saw love—not just God's general love but each part of His brilliance, and it was targeted at revealing Himself to us. Each part of His plan was designed so that someone could walk into the fullness of their original design for eternity. A voice like music came to me and sang or said or whispered, I couldn't tell, "Jesus paid a price so you could see this, so you could correct every place that broke love. Everyone who walks with Me will bring the world into transformation and back to our intention. Jesus made a way for you to enter here."

"Where am I?" I asked.

"In the Father's heart, in His mind. You are at rest in His Spirit. You are in Me." Wave after wave of His love came over me.

Then I looked outward from this place, which seemed very far away, to the earth below. I saw the enemy, Satan, and it should have disturbed me to see him while I was in this place, but I was completely at peace within God. I had no fear. I could see all that he was plotting—it looked like spider webs throughout the earth. I felt a burning intensity of God's Father heart all around me. Some of the spider webs looked like they were binding people to sin, to death, to their fallen natures, and I felt the burning again.

"He really hates Satan, doesn't He?" I asked the Spirit.

"You are feeling His burning love for humanity. His heart has jealous anger. His holiness is a burning fire. Jesus paid a price so that every infringement or infraction toward His jealous love would be corrected for those who would embrace Him." I remember hearing that quote from a pastor, but hearing it now from an angel, I knew where it originated.

I felt as though I were in a love-weapons storeroom over a fully weaponized nation like America, and all the weapons felt loaded with love and aimed. I could feel His love, and it seemed like a countdown clock, ready to strike.

"God is a God of justice," I heard all around me, and I knew and could trust that our timeline was being observed by this jealous lover who was ready to rescue and restore everything that was lost. No one was getting away with anything. Everything would be judged. *Every injustice would have a redemption.*

We are His, not His policemen on the earth. We are His armed forces, armed with love.

It is no mistake that I saw all the cures, schematics, and formulas before I saw this picture of a jealous God who has plans of justice. His brilliance has already made a provision to correct every violation of love, and we are not the policemen of people's carnal nature, nor are we the lawyers against humanity and their activity. We are God's armed forces, armed with the brilliance of His redemptive love that Jesus declared.

> The Spirit of the Lord is upon me, and he has anointed me to be hope for the poor, healing for the brokenhearted, and new eyes for the blind, and to preach to prisoners, "You are set free!" I have come to share the message of Jubilee, for the time of God's great acceptance has begun.
>
> —LUKE 4:18–19

The Spirit said, "You aren't supposed to tell people what they are not and then punish the wicked. That is My job, and I am a jealous God." I felt this delightful being, who had been so soft, turn violent and uncontrollable. It was truly like the picture of the lamb and then the lion in the Bible. The lion was about to roar.

"Your job is to manifest what is in My heart," He said.

"But how?" I thought, and He laughed, and His laugh was like the sound of happy water.

"Look into my Word, look into My heart; sometimes just do the opposite of what you see the enemy doing on the earth. Where the enemy uses world hunger as a weapon, you are supposed to pray into it and help be part of the solution. You have the science straight from our mind, if you would only use your access to apprehend it. When carnal men set up trafficking rings around the world, you don't just want natural justice and jail time for them; you want redemption. You want things to be made right again. You want to bring the education, therapy, and deliverance needed to the world to reveal why trafficking is so evil, and to uproot the unrighteous planting of sin in our cultures that allows so much evil because of selfish lust."

> God did not send his Son into the world to judge and condemn the world, but to be its Savior and rescue it! So now there is no longer any condemnation for those who believe in him, but the unbeliever already lives under condemnation because they do not believe in the name of the only Son of God. And here is the basis for their judgment: The Light of God has now come into the world, but the people loved darkness more than the Light, because they want the darkness to conceal their evil. So the wicked hate the Light and try to hide from it, for the Light fully exposes their lives. But those who love the truth will come into the Light, for the Light will reveal that it was God who produced their fruitful works.
>
> —JOHN 3:17–21

"When you pursue your relationship with God with this view— that His miraculous nature is abiding in you—you are an ark of

His presence amid the enemies of your God, and He will fight through you for what is His. You will begin to anticipate the manifestation of His jealous, miraculous nature from this arsenal of creative brilliance that is within His being.

"Solomon wasn't trying to end all the wars his father had engaged in with neighboring nations by wisdom alone. He was filled with the mind and perceptions of God. He could see what was needed to diffuse each complicated war and each destroyed relationship. He looked into the mind and perceptions of God and didn't just have peace because he was more powerful or wealthy. He had peace that *created* relationship and trade between nations. He was able to accumulate more wealth than anyone else not by barbarian takeovers but by interdependent relationship with God rising up from within his instinct and counsel," the angel said. Then we went back to the place of the original vision.

Unpacking the Box on the Shelf

I was back in the place before time with the angel of God. He showed me a shelf full of boxes of seeds, many of which I saw poured out (in other parts of these visions I have described to you). But then I saw a box of fertilizer. "This is for your time and the time to come," he said.

"Is this the secret sauce of success everyone wants?" I wondered.

The Spirit and the angels of heaven started to take fertilizer from this box and sprinkle it over all the places where He had planted His nature in His people. What struck me is that I wasn't seeing organizations growing or miraculous talents and skills developing. I kept watching. What was this growing?

"Do you want to see?" the angel asked.

Of course I had to see it. What was this? Then I knew it wasn't a thing to see; it was a feeling. Inside of me, in my God wiring to know Him, I could sense what felt like the core of His heart. I could sense what it felt like when the fall of man started. Then I could feel traces of acts of injustice. I am not an overly emotional person, but I was immediately experiencing deep emotions that were extremely uncomfortable.

"You are feeling His miraculous compassion for the people who experienced injustice, people He knew before time began. This compassion is now being imparted in a way that no generation has been able to fully see to date. In this time, the enemy is working toward owning a worldwide connection through technology and even globalization, but God is the author of it all. He is fertilizing a generation who can help start implementing the plans of His heart because they are aware and activated with His heart."

When so many in charismatic and Pentecostal churches think about heaven invading earth, they think of the miraculous and signs and wonders, direct evangelism and missionization; they think of church planting and activities that are demonstrated in the church and by Christians. These are all obviously good and real and needed. They are things we are very familiar with. We want to build with God, for God, His church among His believers. The catalyst, though, for the growth Jesus was promised from the Father was not centered in these activities alone (although, again, these activities would never cease to be important). God's justice and advancement is *also* about bringing transformation in *all* the quadrants of society. His purposes are not only about bringing people out of darkness and into the light but also about developing what the kingdom of God looks like here.

I saw into people's hearts in our generation and, increasingly, in every future generation before His return. They were being sprinkled with compassion in so many areas. Everything—from human rights to agricultural and food systems, environmentalism to social justice, global prison reform all the way to children in warzones—was being reframed with a kingdom perspective. So many areas were being populated with Christian thinking because of the heavenly fertilizer that was planted for our generation. It will be the catalyst for growth in the move of God.

"In your generation, God has created people to be apostles or leaders in every place that can be reconnected to God's original plan," the angel said. "God is sending the engineers of transformation on a great deployment."

I knew that it was going to be messy but beautiful, like the birth of a child.

CHAPTER 11

GOD'S ORIGINAL INTENTION

L ooking at these billions of humans tied to the heartstrings of God, pulsating with His spiritual neurons and ready to become brilliant carriers of His glorious nature, was breathtaking. But then it was hard because I live in our timeline. I thought, "I see so much brokenness here. We have walked away from this beautifully crafted master plan for so long. So much has fallen short of what God dreamed."

"All has fallen short of what He dreamed," the angel said. "Man left the garden, the earth started to die, and humanity has done more to destroy the earth than to redeem it. But let me show you..." He took my hand, and I had a vision of the most important moment to humanity in history besides its creation.

THE HEAVENLY RIPPLE

I saw Jesus again, this time at the very point of death on the cross. When He died, a ripple went out through everything He created. Every cell in every human's body, every part of every animal, the earth itself, the angels, and every star flickered with a new purpose. Something new was set in motion, and everything had His layer of glory all over it. It permeated everywhere and everything. How could this be when we had been so far apart from God, and now the gap between heaven and earth felt so thin? His purpose was in every corner of the universe. How could that previously vast separation suddenly feel one step from being reconnected in *every* situation? How could the broken fragmentation over the earth, food, plants, animals, humans, and systems of man be so close to being completed again? It was like everything was on the verge of its own great tipping point of re-creation. This is what Jesus had been revealing in His life: the restoration of all things,

> that He may send [to you] Jesus, the Christ, who has been appointed for you, whom heaven must keep until the time for the [complete] restoration of all things about which God promised through the mouth of His holy prophets from ancient time.
>
> —ACTS 3:20–21, AMP

"From that day [when Jesus died]," the angel said, "all of heaven has been at work to redeem and restore all things back to God's original intention so that Jesus can have the fullness of what He paid a price for—complete connection to His original plan in its new version."

> We look at this Son and see the God who cannot be seen. We look at this Son and see God's original purpose in everything created. For everything, absolutely everything, above and below, visible and invisible, rank after rank after rank of angels—everything got started in him and finds its purpose in him. He was there before any of it came into existence and holds it all together right up to this moment. And when it comes to the church, he organizes and holds it together, like a head does a body....So spacious is he, so expansive, that everything of God finds its proper place in him without

crowding. Not only that, but all the broken and dislocated pieces of the universe—people and things, animals and atoms—get properly fixed and fit together in vibrant harmonies, all because of his death, his blood that poured down from the cross.

—Colossians 1:15–20, MSG

"Everything you are seeing in what was, from the beginning of eternity, has the full potential to be restored or redeemed again," the angel said.

Hope flooded me. Jesus hadn't just been resurrected; He had torn the veil between Himself and us. Now everything felt so close to Him, yet in my natural life I had often said, "Everything feels so far away from God's plan." This revelation was like seeing the northern lights in a dark sky—I was filled with awe and wonder. I couldn't deny the power of His light in darkness. It was all-consuming to my vision.

"Look!" The angel pointed, and I saw heaven, and in the center was a light brighter than the sun. It was so bright I couldn't look at it fully. I tried to cover my face and see through the gap in my fingers, but it was of no use.

"That is Him resurrected!" And I knew that His light was more brilliant than a thousand suns. He was holding in His hands the keys to everything—the keys to get it all back, the keys to the full recovery. There is no mistake that heaven doesn't need a sun because Jesus shines far more brilliantly.

Then I looked at my hands and body, and I too looked like a being of light. I felt very practical and whole, even though it was more of a mystical experience. "You are a carrier of the light of the world. Go forth and shine." Jesus' words vibrated through my cells. I couldn't imagine ever being in a dark room again; I was so bright. I looked over the earth, and there again were those points of light everywhere, creating the great net or root system of the glory of God that canopied the earth.

What Was in Darkness

Then the angel said, "Look!" And I knew that it was real time in my age, while I was alive, yet it was beyond what I was seeing. Pulsating light was coming from heaven and hitting that net of connected lights—all the believers who were in faith on the earth—and it looked like neurons were firing and then working through a neurological MRI. These lights were hitting the earth— not only coming into believers but blanketing the entire earth. The lights were His ultimate truths about love, peace, righteousness, and holiness. It sounds like such a religious picture if you are disconnected from those words, but He showed me how to make it spiritually practical.

One of the light waves that canopied the earth held in it the truth of humanity's right to freedom. It hit so strongly that it started to dislodge racial issues, slavery, gender inequality, children at risk, and more. It was like a wave of the truth in His being, about how He created us, was globalized for all of us to partake from, even if we had grown up thinking differently. This truth became sparks of ideas of freedom and justice all around the earth regarding the rights God has designed His creation to have.

It was overwhelming. I thought, "Surely this is the end times," because the truth was so strong and had never been revealed in such a full way. When you look at history, there has never been a time when people tried to bring alignment to all these issues such as women's rights, anti-human trafficking or anti-slavery, racial civil rights, and so on. It's been an amazing time to be alive!

But as I watched, something happened as people grabbed hold of the truth. Some people who weren't saved, and some people who were saved, were creating information—a case—around the truth so they could justify their wrong lifestyles or their lesser choices. They gave themselves rights that God never intended or created humans to have. The enemy was like a mastermind behind this strategy, and I cried out "No!" because I was so concerned with how truth was being misrepresented as it was being released on the globe. Extreme forms of perverted social justice were rallied around as the ultimate way to express the truths that were being given freely by God.

"God is allowing truth to be distributed and seen all over the earth in a way that will give people a choice," the angel said. "He always gives His nature freely, and He allows humanity to choose if they want to partner with Him in it. He will only abide in the truth that expresses His love, though. Everything else will not last." The angel was trying to comfort me, and it was powerful to think that our God would rather give us truth and wisdom than mature humanity—so that we can have even greater options and ways to choose Him, even if it means we might choose ourselves and be even more evil.

I compare it to being in the 1950s when the food system was awakened in America. We were going to have shortages, yet we had the technology and the agricultural ability to feed the world. So many corporations ended up perverting the truth: America had a calling to lead in the food systems of the world, yet they prostituted and perverted the whole thing by raping our soil, creating harmful agriculture with a wrong use of chemicals and overusing GMOs, and even raising livestock unethically. We are still paying for this fifty-plus years later. We can stop there and mourn, or we can look at the potential of what regenerative agriculture and healthy corporations are doing. They are promoting the ethical use of livestock and passing laws that are positioned to create a true healthy and organic narrative. All of that came out of a food awareness that not many had before, except a few people groups who lived directly off the land.

More of God's brilliant truth was being released over areas of agricultural technology, transportation, government, education, and entertainment. Almost everywhere I looked, I could see His original thoughts and His spiritual neurons of fullness being released onto the earth and causing a response in some of humanity—just like in Solomon.

Then I saw some extremely targeted light waves from His Spirit over people groups, and the light contained His original intention. "Part of the great maturing of resources I showed you, that God prepared before the beginning of time and is maturing now, is the resource on how to use this truth. It will help whole people groups have freedom, resources, and identity for their purpose for now and the end of the age."

I didn't really understand, and I wanted to ask a million questions, but I heard something like a sonic boom and saw four light waves of truth blanket the earth. It was like watching nuclear explosions from His heart. Everything within the blast radius wasn't destroyed but imprinted by the truth. I could probably write a whole book on these four waves, but I will try and do it justice through this chapter.

Sonic Boom 1: The Asian Blessing

The first wave I saw was over Asians. Oh, how God loves Asians. He had planned the densest population of Asians in history to be in this generation. He had planned this group to be one of the saving graces of humanity. He had hidden so much in them when it comes to the mysteries of building, technology, agriculture, servanthood, leadership, art, expression. I mean, I know we were all created equally, but both individually and by culture and race, we all have different appointments and purposes and redemptive gifts. Can you imagine seeing what I was seeing—God's love for an entire race that He had redemptively planned? In the center of this truth was the fact that Asians would become the dominant race group on the earth to help usher in the full coming of Jesus. That doesn't mean any other race is irrelevant or not as important, but God put something in the Asian people to enable them to multiply and expand because He knew they would be the ones, in the end, who would pray without ceasing until His return—like no other people group except the Jews.

I saw some Asian nations that would begin to understand God's love for Israel, and I saw many Asian nations having companies in Israel. I felt that there would be entire cities built by the wealth of Asian nations, and it would bring a new measure of economy to Israel.

I saw the revival that would happen first among Asian people and then from Asia reach back to the West. It wasn't achieved through traditional missions when it departed Asian nations, but it was just as powerful or more so. I saw Asian men and women being made Josephs in places of influence, and they had favor and excellence. They were being positioned at key times over financial markets, disaster preparedness organizations, agriculture, and tech industries. They were going to be some of God's saving grace to humanity in those positions, as their calling and appointment was from God.

SONIC BOOM 2: THE DREAD CHAMPIONS LED BY BLACK COMMUNITIES IN AMERICA AND THE UK

The Lord is with me as a dread champion [one to be greatly feared]; therefore my persecutors will stumble and not overcome [me]. They will be completely shamed, for they have not acted wisely and have failed [in their schemes]; their eternal dishonor will never be forgotten.

—JEREMIAH 20:11, AMP

Dread champions were the "champions" for the king during the time of chivalry. Being chosen as the dread champion, or one others dreaded to fight because of their abilities and reputation, was a great honor for a knight, as he was chosen by the king to represent the region or nation the king controlled.

The dread champion fought for the king and the country, usually in individual battles or in a contest against the champion of another king. Whichever champion won the battle of war or contest, that nation won the territory or people being fought over.

Using the dread champion in a war also saved many lives, as others would not have to fight. People would believe that God was with the dread champion who won.

Bob Jones had a vision of this before he died. In a prophetic word posted online in 2010, Jones wrote:

> Recently the Lord showed me great trees that touched Heaven in their time. The Lord cut them down and made pulpwood out of them. Then they were put into press and made into scrolls. The Bible is their testimony. They were "dread champions" in their times; they championed the cause for the Lord. They left a great inheritance for us, because without us they couldn't be made perfect.
>
> And all of these, though they won divine approval by [means of] their faith, did not receive the fulfillment of what was promised, because God had us in mind and had something better and greater in view for us, so that they [these heroes and heroines of faith] should not come to perfection apart from us [before we could join them].
>
> —HEBREWS 11:39–40, AMP

The Holy Spirit is calling for those who would champion His cause to grow up, and to touch heaven and champion His cause in their lifetimes. These are the dread champions who will stand up against the enemy, like these mighty champions of the past did in their time. They left us a legacy!

Now let us take up our cross and follow Him, beginning where these dread champions left off. "Save and help and rescue, LORD, for godly people cease to be, for the faithful vanish from among the sons of men" (Ps. 12:1, AMP). Their lives are now scrolls written in the Word of God for our instruction.

The Lord is raising up other dread champions to champion his cause, like David, who was a dread champion.

Once You spoke in a vision to Your devoted ones and said, I have endowed one who is mighty [a hero, giving him the power to help—to be a champion for Israel]; I have exalted one chosen from among the people. I have found David My servant; with My holy oil have I anointed him.

—PSALM 89:19–20, AMPC

The Lord asked me to ask for three things. On July 3, 1984, the Lord visited me for half an hour. He asked me to pray scriptures to Him and ask for three things. The Lord said He would answer them in that order.

- The first thing I prayed was Psalm 12:1 (quoted previously).

- The second thing I prayed for was help for the church to overcome their unbelief so that their faith would not fail.

- The third thing I prayed for was power.

I believe that we have already seen the Lord answer the first two things I prayed for. Now we are getting ready for the third answer to take place.[1]

God is releasing these dread champions in the African and Black communities, especially in Europe, in America, and, of course, in Africa. In the vision was a militancy for God's justice and righteousness or rightness. I knew God was going to bring His anointing on issues like civil rights in places like America, but that wasn't the focus of this empowerment. God was putting on this people group a violent warrior spirit that was going to fight for the manifestation of the kingdom in places where it had been locked up or was being threatened.

I saw the Black church in the UK rising up against radicalized political ideals, and I saw Black men and women being raised up to be leaders in parliament. I saw a Black leader becoming the prime minister, and he was listening to Christian church leaders and helping to sway the scales away from moral bankruptcy.

I saw God lancing a wound of racism and political racial agenda in America, after a great explosion of it, so that several movements would be led by Christian Black leaders to restore God's purpose in education, religious reform in government, and human rights.

I saw God raising up South Africa as a key developed nation that would lead other African nations out of third-world status (out of example or help), and also help show what a developed African nation—that follows a Western model in trade, manufacturing, and government—looks like.

SONIC BOOM 3: THE ARMY LED BY CHILDREN

Then I saw a vast army of indescribable numbers, but as I zoomed in I realized the average age of a soldier in it was around twelve. What was I seeing? This army descended on the moral decay on the earth and raised their weapons over injustice. There were so many of them I couldn't find their end. Then I looked at the army of the enemy, and it was small in comparison, so small they didn't have a chance.

"Who are these warrior children?" I asked the angel.

He showed me one of their hearts, and it was expanded. It was so large. Then I saw Jesus, but He wasn't the young man in His thirties. He was twelve. He was ready to go into His Father's house. His faith was strong and activated. I flashed forward to see these children again and realized they had the same activation of truth that Jesus had had at twelve.

The science behind the twelve-year-old

When we look at what is happening with twelve-year-olds, it's amazing. Right now, the average age of people who get saved is younger than twelve. It's an astounding fact, but children who meet Jesus have so much going on in them. I once heard they have more neurons firing in their brains between the ages of eleven and thirteen than at any other time in their lives. That is why you can visually picture your high school crush even better than you can your college crush. Children's brains are developing at the speed of light, or with increased neurons. Barna argues that a child's moral development is set by the age of nine, but there is very little focus on children of this age.[2]

Why is this important? It's another way that God wired humanity.

What is the most oppressed people group in the world? It is not a nation, like the war-torn Congo. It is not a racial group within a divisive nation or a religiously persecuted group occupying space with another religious group. It is far and wide understood to be children. Why is this? Because childhood is the age span for when God wires most people to meet Him and follow Him. Many theologians believe a lot of the disciples were teenagers. Almost all theologians recognize that Mary was a young teen.

The enemy knows what will happen if the church focuses resources and training downward, and so we have been stuck with giving children a less-powerful form of Christianity with no graduation process into having "real" impact through their faith.

God is going to raise up children's ministries with national and global impact.

There is about to be a commissioning for media, ministries, and educational programs, along with games, video games, and online social platforms, to help kids become true disciples. There will be literally billions of dollars and incredible resources that go into the formation of this children's army.

SONIC BOOM 4: THE TIME OF GREAT DISCERNMENT

The angel who had just shown me all of these things looked at me with the sternness of a PhD-level instructor at an Ivy League school. "You live in the age of information and knowledge, and what will set you apart is the discernment of Solomon."

Out of all the things that would set us apart, I didn't expect Him to say "discernment." I expected the power of Elijah or the ability to raise up people to hear God like Samuel or the apostolic anointing of Paul. But instead He contrasted it to discernment.

The angel grabbed my shoulder and said, "Let me show you."

CHAPTER 12

DISCERNING THE HEAVENLY REALMS

THE ANGEL TOOK me to the heavenly realms and said, "Part of the great maturing will be in Christians' ability to discern. I will show you things that will help you understand your enhanced access to the Father's discernment [that you were born with] when you became reborn."

I felt filled with an inquisitive mind, like a kindergartner's, and wanted to ask hours' worth of questions, and the angel had not even shown me anything yet. Even knowing that part of the work of the Spirit of God was to give me a curious, childlike heart was a message to me. I had not been curious enough, and I wanted to remember this moment. Curiosity takes energy, and my life was so full of responsibility that I had not wanted to spend extra energy—especially on mystery—in the past season.

THE FIRST HEAVEN

I felt like Superman as my eyes and senses flew around the earth, watching it in a time lapse. I got to see how it was originally, and I was in awe. I was crying and laughing in wonder. Have you ever been somewhere so beautiful that your senses were overwhelmed, but in the best possible way? I stared at Niagara Falls and felt the power of its sound in my chest and watched as it beat down on the waters below. I viewed the rustic jungles of the Amazon and walked for hours without coming to the end of new sights, sounds, creatures, and bugs (I didn't like the bugs). After I finished, exhausted, I was imprinted with the memories forever. I can still close my eyes fifteen-plus years later and see the sights I saw those days because they marked me so much.

Seeing earth in its original state before the fall is like watching thousands of master artists doing their craft at once, and it wasn't just breathtaking; I could have lived there forever and forgotten everything else. I understood why God, the master Creator, took rest in it and enjoyed it. It was so worthy, so holy, so wonderful.

Then the angel started to allow what I was seeing to time lapse, so I could see different marks in time, after the fall, of what had progressed and regressed upon the earth. Seeing it all through God's eyes, I had compassion for the way the environment was affected. It was never supposed to suffer from the particular energy types we have chosen to create and use, such as manufactured plastics and papers. We have destroyed entire sections of creation that God never intended to be used that way. Human waste was causing whole areas that I was enjoying in the beginning to become unrecognizable because of the destruction.

It was heartbreaking to realize that a lot of the ways we have used the earth's resources don't go along with how God designed it for us. Can you imagine if we were as excited to know His heart in regard to energy production as we were over building larger church campuses? A large church may last a decent amount of time, but His energy plans would last until His return, if we could just discern what was in His original plan.

I started to see the impact of bad plastics and how they had poisoned entire sections of the earth and its oceans, but beyond the plastic and the problem, I saw a spark in my mind's eye. As I focused on it, I saw several types of resources and inventions that were His pure designs, His original intentions. These were more practical, helpful, and just plain easy to mold, reuse, and repurpose than traditional plastic. It was amazing! The design is there, in His mind, for someone to grab. What traditional plastic has meant to humanity for convenience, these new materials will mean so much more. They could take us into a whole new era of building—everything from cars, planes, and food products to even huge structures like dams and bridges—with little to no effect on the soil, trash system, or emissions issues with their creation. I was in awe, and it hit me. "This is available, isn't it?" I asked the angel.

"It has been available, but someone needs to connect with God's jealous heart of love over the earth and dream His thoughts with Him." The angel looked sad, yet I could see the wonder in his eyes about these things.

Then I looked again over the whole earth and saw all the living things and animals. Wow! What a source of God's joy in the creative genius of each creature, each botanical system, the whole ecosystem itself. He was so proud of it, so in love with it.

Then I saw an animal at a certain time cease to exist, because when the fall happened, the earth began to derail from His original plan of life. Oxygen got less dense, animals began to rely on each other as food sources, and the process of natural selection and the food chain started to happen. Angels wept at this day, much like we would weep if we watched a movie that had violating scenes in it. It wasn't how God intended it, and it was brutal.

I don't know that the angels around God have ever adjusted to this fallen state of the world; they are as eager as He is for its restoration. Picture the most empathetic, compassionate person you know, one so sensitive that when someone else's child dies, they identify and feel pain in it, even if they don't know the person. God's dreams looked like they were dying on the earth. God's beautiful creation, the only thing they had ever watched His heart come alive for on this level, was descending from its glory. Angels wept. It happens. They didn't know God's full plan, but they trusted He had one.

As the angel and I continued to look at the earth's time lapse, I saw humanity growing after the fall and spreading to every corner of the earth. Some groups did better than others with how they interacted with God's glorious gift of living creation. For example, many indigenous people had a level of honor for the earth and creation, and they felt the holiness of God, even if they didn't understand who He was. Then I saw the modernization and advancements. All advancement was inspired by God's nature in humanity, yet so much of it was warped and had twisted away from the original seed of God's holy purpose that had been placed inside of us. Whole industries felt inspired by God but not inhabited by His presence, which would have caused them to come into glory.

It was so wonderful to watch man yet so heartbreaking. The same glorious nature God created inside of them, based on His own, caused them to build cities that were stunning displays of ingenuity, but then they destroyed them because of their own sinful battles and politics. The same humans who were partnering with God's desire to bring healing were creating science to destroy diseases, yet then creating diseases to harness their power. It was all so confusing, but it was relatable to my heart because of my own fallen humanity—one I am so glad is being purged out of me as I am discipled by this God of love.

THE GLORY OF GOD

> But what happens when we live God's way? He brings gifts into our lives, much the same way that fruit appears in an orchard—things like affection for others, exuberance about life, serenity. We develop a willingness to stick with things, a sense of compassion in the heart, and a conviction that a basic holiness permeates things and people.
>
> —GALATIANS 5:22–23, MSG

As the vision turned to these modern times, the one thing I noticed was that I could see the same glory that was in the beginning, before the fall, all over the earth. The same presence of God's awesome design and nature that He wove into everything was still permeating every people group and place. Even if it was being misused, God wasn't removing His basic glory. Even in humanity, He wasn't stripping them of the free gift of the image and dream He had for each one of them. There were stunning things hidden inside of humans that were just there and part of God.

We are like arks built to carry the presence of God, yet for so many humans the presence isn't there. The ark could be filled with a lot of different things, but many trash this beautiful image of God while others use it for their own purposes.

But then I saw them—the most glorious beings—and I thought I had fast-forwarded to the end times or to after the return of Jesus. I saw these amazing, intricately made arks inside of glorious people who were filled with the presence of God, and they could do *anything*. I mean, they were not limited to their humanity because they had so become carriers of the glory of God that anything was possible to them. The structure built around their faith carried God's heart, mind, and perceptions, and when they looked out on the earth, they could see through the lens of His dreams and heart. They allowed themselves to be unlimited because they were living out of His vision.

It was as if the Bible were heavily memorized in their minds, and their spirits were filled with the stories of who God is and what He can do, both biblically and through the testimonies they'd heard. They had a gift to absorb testimonies of how God manifested through believers, both past and present, and this became their prototype, and in that they became some of the greatest people of faith the world had ever known.

It was strange because they were looking around our earthly realm and seeing things in the other realms as well, and that made me so much more curious. "Where are they looking?" I thought. The angel touched my head, and I saw.

The Second Heaven

The angel with me put his hands over my eyes, opening me up to something that was so familiar but so new at the same time. "God created a space between heaven and earth that is the place where angels were always intended to interact and be at work. It's not that it was ever supposed to be invisible, per se, to man; it was supposed to be looked at through the connected eyes of love with God so that it could be understood. God never intended that we angels be a butler service to you. He created us more as beautiful stewards of all that He created. Like the human body has billions of cells that work in harmony to define and help its living system, angels are like beautiful living cells that make up the system of creation, working together to keep His will and connection going forward."

I could see just that. This spiritual plane looked like it was an intricate communication sector between God's nature in heaven and the earthly realm I could see. It didn't look like sci-fi or fantasy in my imagination but rather a very clear process that would make sense even in the natural if we had the right science or understanding. It was more brilliant than anything I had seen on the earth.

As I looked around, things would overlap from this place to the earth, almost as if you could draw a curtain and see the visible realm instantly. I wanted to see Los Angeles from this place because I love it so much. We looked at it spiritually, and it was wild! I looked down at Hollywood, one of my favorite areas, and I could see that in this realm all history was imprinted on it—almost like a digital map. I could see everyone who ever lived there, their history and impact on everyone else, and everything that had ever happened. All information was presented here like an instantly accessible historical database. History couldn't be hidden, both good and bad. I looked at one living person, and I could see the root system of their history. I looked down long lines of their life and saw everything about them, every choice they had made, the parents and relationships they came from, even their country of origin. Then I could see that country's origin.

The information held here was so exhausting to my mind that I closed my eyes. "Everything that has ever happened in your timeline is imprinted here," the angel said, smiling, and I realized that in this place between heaven and earth, history itself was unveiled and powerful but also tragic and broken. I felt overwhelmed by it. I guess I thought, as a Western world human, that most of what happens in our life, our choices, and our history wasn't that important and was just gone after it happened. But when I looked here, I could see how every choice created its own root system, which would inspire new choices, even if they were not good ones.

I could see entire issues over America and where they had started. It's not that I could ever articulate what I was seeing, but just as Adam and Eve made a very clear choice that led us here, I could see other choices different people had made that empowered much evil and derailed us from God's master plan. I could feel the hope of God's heart in this, but I couldn't see it in the structure of what I was looking at. History, the way I was seeing it, seemed ugly.

"You are looking and then trying to process with your humanity rather than with His Spirit that He gave you. That is how most believers discern here." The angel had compassion on me, but I didn't yet understand what he was saying.

"I have to show you more."

THE DEMONIC OVERLAP OF THIS REALM

But then the angel showed me the lowest parts of this place, so darkened and corrupted. There were completely red spots, like blood clots, in the arteries of the universe, almost as if you were looking at an MRI and saw cancer or tumors. I knew it wasn't how it was supposed to be. "What am I seeing?"

"When Satan was thrown down from heaven with all of his usurping army, they were never allowed to go back to heaven, nor are they allowed to fully visit earth...except through possessing man. They are at work here, trying to use all information against God and man, trying to accumulate power through manipulation and the greed to destroy. Where you are seeing darkness is where they are using humanity against itself. There is where humans have come into agreement with the enemy. Those are the places where hell is ruling through humanity." He looked disgusted.

I had a sudden awareness, though, that it didn't look as bad as I'd thought it would. Here I was, in this vast spiritual place so full of the heavenly purpose of God, being transported by the heavenly host. It was so full of His Spirit. I had always pictured this place to be like a haunted house or a dark void of demonic existence only. Instead it felt like 95 percent of it was the body of the whole universe working perfectly toward the return of Jesus, with only 5 percent corrupted. That corruption was wreaking havoc on the rest of the system, but to see the 95 percent so healthy, so purposeful, was such a different perspective.

"When Jesus restored all things at the cross, we won, and this realm has been fully His," the angel said. "He has the keys to heaven, earth, the spirit realm, death, and life—*it's all His.*" I knew what he was saying wasn't meant to rebuke me, but I was convicted by how much power I had let my imagination give the enemy. Compared to what had been imparted with my Christianity, I knew the superstition over what could and couldn't bring spiritual oppression to me was extremely exaggerated when I saw how little power the enemy had.

It's like that, though, in the world. Having gone into red-light districts, war zones, places where communism was falling or where gangs were oppressing, I know that evil is imposed by a small group of falsely empowered people who terrorize the masses. If you think about the fact that only one-third of the angels went with the usurper, the odds of heaven winning battles are crazy. Not only are angels two-to-one to demons, but the angels have all the power, glory, and creative nature of God behind them. The enemy has been stripped of every part of God's creative design and ability. He has *no power* except to try and possess it from living humans.

"The enemy cannot create anymore," the angel said. "The enemy isn't like a comic supervillain with superpowers; he has cunning and a destructive vendetta against humanity *with very little power left.*"

THE IMPRISONED

Like much of this book, you can read what I am about to share as a parable. It is extra-biblical but will help you have faith in the nature of God, even if it's not literal. It comes from experiential truth that can be supported by the Bible, but it does not have to define your theology.

Jude 6 says,

> In the same way, there were heavenly messengers in rebellion who went outside their rightful domain of authority and abandoned their appointed realms. God bound them in everlasting chains and is keeping them in the dark abyss of the netherworld until the judgment of the great day.

One thing I had never known is that since the fall of man, the fallen angels have been increasingly imprisoned. We see this referred to in Jude 6–7; 1 Peter 3:18–20; and 2 Peter 2:4–7; and we also see this in the Apocrypha and in extra-biblical accounts of angels and demons throughout history, but now I was seeing it.

In this spiritual realm, I could see a place right at the edge of space and time that the Bible calls hell or hades. It was a place void of God's nature, His likeness, His goodness, His glory. It was a place guarded by just two cherubim, much like the cherubim guarded the Garden of Eden. They were protecting man from going back into the garden, but in this place the angels were protecting what was inside this sphere from coming out.

Now picture yourself as an angel who can steward the creative nature of God—connecting His eternal glory to the whole created world, unfolding time and space, man and animal, earth and planets. Then you rebel and God strips all your ability to connect to His nature. What is left? Because God created everything with its own singular identity, you are now an angel without a purpose, without a cause, without a balance to goodness, without hope, without truth. You have the shell of the body you were created in without God's nature inspiring it. Picture having a disease where your healthy cells all die and get corrupted. It's even worse than that because every cell of their being is separated from God.

God is the Spirit of truth, so from this point on no truth can ever be understood by the framing of God's consciousness, which completes all things, because the fallen angels don't have the mind for it. These were the ones imprisoned in this place. In the middle of this place I could barely look into was a lake of holy fire. It was the final resting place reserved for the end of time for every being that was there.

My mind was asking how, what, and why at the same time, and it was painful. "Those fallen angels that are there were imprisoned, never to come out again," the angel said.

"I don't understand. Why weren't they all imprisoned from the time of the fall?"

"Because God wanted man to help Him judge them," the angel replied. "And man has been doing that ever since the return of Christ—over regions, over systems, over families. More and more fallen angels have been imprisoned since the time of Noah, and half the population is in there now."

"I still don't understand," I said.

"Jesus came to restore all things. Part of His restoration plan is to give the kingdom and the power over the enemy's kingdom to man. When He said what you bind on earth is bound in heaven, He meant it. When man restores God's original plan and intention over an area, the demons have no power there and are imprisoned. They have no more rights there."

I was confused but in awe. Could this be real? Could half of the demonic army already be imprisoned, awaiting the final judgment day?

"Think about how much human sacrifice was rampant on the earth in so many cultures. When human beings chose, as a greater whole, that the life of humanity had sanctity, most of the demons behind this were not just put out of commission; the Spirit of truth blocked them from having a role on the earth anymore and they were imprisoned. Yes, there are still demons behind human sacrifice, and some have actually become generals for the abortionist cause in the spirit, but as man makes higher choices to align with the truth of God, these demons are displaced and imprisoned.

"This is one of the ways that man can judge even the fallen angels and demons. He displaces the works of the devil, and so the devils are imprisoned because they have no opening left to operate among the humans. When Jesus cast out demons, He didn't cast them back into the spirit realm to have their way, He cast them to hell where they belong. Their works are no longer flourishing among man. They don't get reincarnated for more sinister purposes."

I thought about this. "When we see so much evil on the earth, like we do now, how can it be true that there are fewer demons at work?"

"In the great maturing that is happening with God's plans right now, He is releasing more of the knowledge that He had designed for humanity and for the world on the earth. He is freely giving this knowledge, knowing that when someone enters into a life in and through Christ, they will use this knowledge mixed with His nature and glory, and it will bring about the return of His investment. Some of the knowledge gets corrupted by man's fallen nature, and that is where the demonic is not just inspired but empowered. These become the seedbeds of evil and destruction. If there is more knowledge and wisdom being given than ever before, there is so much more at stake. If the demons can control it, the damage is even greater."

I was so concerned, but he smiled, took me up higher, and showed me again how 95 percent of this place was occupied by

God's activity. "For to us a child is born, to us a son is given, and the government will be on his shoulders. And he will be called Wonderful Counselor, Mighty God, Everlasting Father, Prince of Peace. Of the greatness of his government and peace there will be no end" (Isa. 9:6–7, NIV). The angel had quoted the prophet Isaiah speaking a prophetic word about the Messiah. "His government has only been growing since He gave it to people like you to increase."

I felt such a mystery of hope in his words.

CHAPTER 13

SEEING WISDOM

"**W**HY DON'T WE see into this place? So much more could happen if we understood how God is working both on earth and in the spiritual realm," I said.

"All humans were hardwired to discern the spiritual realm in some way or another," the angel said. "You were designed with spiritual genius inside of you, but the world puts you through a system of stripping all faith and shutting down your spiritual senses, or perverting them, from the time you are young. The enemy tries to create distractions to what this place is and raises up false spiritual expressions to mimic what the realm of the spirit is like." He walked toward me and smiled.

"But God has wired in man the ability to see and know what He is doing through us here. You just have to let Him open your spiritual senses—the ones He created you with—and look, smell, hear, taste, and feel through His Spirit."

I could see so many things at once through God's eyes. It was like scriptures that were imprinted in my spirit were being quoted a hundred at a time, they were so alive here. I compared it to when

Luke was writing his Gospel and kept referring to how Jesus was the fulfillment of all the Old Testament messianic prophecies. I could see the fulfillment of all of Scripture here. My mind was supercharged, but I knew not how all of it would remain in my conscious thinking when I came out of the vision.

Then my spiritual sense of feeling was front and center. I could feel God's plans and heartbeat. I could sense His will over a particular human I was looking at from this realm. I could see all the resources coming from heaven in this place, and I knew everything they needed for the fullness of what He had called them to was right within spiritual reach. I could discern their gifts, their calling, the relationships God was bringing them. I could feel His love nature for them, and it was so intense and full.

While all this was happening, I could also feel the angels shooting by me—as if I were in the busiest intersection of Los Angeles—and they were preparing every good thing for the people I was witnessing. They were moving behind them for protection, helping the world around them to not be the destructive, ticking time bomb that the fall had once made it. Instead they were preparing it as the feast of God's very nature that the Trinity had created it to be.

I wanted to see everything here! But then, out of the corner of my eye, I saw something that made me so sad.

I saw a woman on earth, sitting across a table from a man who marketed himself as a psychic medium. He was born, like all of us, with a connection to the spiritual realm, but he did not know Jesus so he couldn't access it with God's thoughts, mind, or intention. He only saw sometimes into the spiritual realm, discerned sometimes the history that was imprinted, or some of the things that were happening. Some of the information he saw was really powerful, but I couldn't see it working within him or spreading to the people he shared it with. Knowledge is power, and this spiritual knowledge was almost intoxicating to him. We were made to see, to know, to feel, but he wasn't accessing it in a connected way that could bring God's perceptions to his knowledge.

It reminded me of reading all you can about a celebrity on the internet and being an expert on their life, their choices, and their family history, but you have never met them. You might be called on by the media to make predictions about them or to write a biography. But you would never be a true expert on the reality of who they are because when you are this far removed from relationship, all you have is information and perhaps some predictions that are closer to being speculation.

This woman who had come to him had lost her husband—and her will to live. Out of desperation, she set up an appointment with this man, a psychic medium, and he was going to do a reading for her.

He told her things about her husband—what his favorite food was, what his last meaningful talk with his daughter was. All of these were written in the history of the spiritual realm. They were good things and true things, but they were just pieces of information that he framed with his narrative. They didn't move her forward, although they encouraged her human heart. They didn't resolve anything. She was still sad, even with the encouragement the information seemed to give her. She still had the trauma of loss; she still only had hope that she would see him again. But she also had some seeds that were half-truths, and they were not causing her to live in hope in life; they were causing her to want more spiritual information.

"Information without relationship is a prison, like death itself," the angel said. "This man is accessing the spiritual realm without relationship with his Creator. The least consequences will be the lack of a fulfilling relationship on his spiritual journey. He'll always be on the outside of the deeper part of what he is seeing, discerning, or interpreting because he doesn't have a living relationship to God.

"The worst consequences of his practice of seeing in this spiritual realm are that he will be consistently manipulated by the demons who live to imitate humans. They show up as false spirits and as the ghosts of those who have gone on so they can keep people from an eternal consciousness and focus on their natural lives."

I knew this meant that if the demonic could imitate a ghost of someone, or give true information with a little false spiritual information, it could keep people stuck in their present circumstances—not offering hope of becoming more, changing them, or challenging their way of thinking, living, loving, or moving on.

I could see many people who were born to be prophets but were afflicted by their gifts because they weren't rooted in relationship to Jesus. It would be like seeing a nine-year-old hearing about all the abuse they had ever experienced and all the pain they had. The child would not be able to handle the information because they would have no way to process it, except to try and come up with some sort of formula or help based on the information.

I was so sad that so many people were being exploited.

Then I saw something even worse. There were people who were doing everything they could, and offering anything they had, to have access to the spiritual realm or the second heavens because they wanted the advantages they misperceived were there. They wanted to be empowered with the knowledge there; they wanted a spiritual relationship to beings that were just angels of light or demons, but they mistook them for enlightened beings.

They were practicing false empowerment and trying to access things that were forbidden by Scripture in the hope of gaining some advantage. Many thought the benefit of helping the world was greater than the sacrifice it took to get the power. The sacrifice was being possessed by the will of the enemy, or a demon itself, so the time they had on earth was not only squandered; they became a pawn in a losing battle.

I could see thousands of years of false spiritual practice that all led to such a lower place in the heavenly realms of the second heavens. Practicing seeing without the discernment of God leading them trapped so many, and it would even create mental illness because people were exposed to spiritual realities that their minds couldn't comprehend or handle.

The Discerners of God's Spirit

Then I saw a different scenario of a teenage girl praying for her friend. Her friend had just opened up about being physically hurt by her boyfriend. God sparked in this girl the ability to see her friend's history. The young girl who was being abused was used to the abuse because she came from a verbally abusive father and had a distorted view of love.

This praying girl saw her history in the spirit realm but with God's perceptions. She saw God's intention over this girl and realized she was going to have to deal with a stronghold of past relationship abuse to help her see the truth of her current situation.

She spoke out of God's intention for her, which was prophetic or foretelling, not just of her future but of God's desire for her: "God has an amazing, loving husband for you, but you will keep getting trapped if you don't allow God to heal your heart of your father's abuse."

This was a spiritual arrow into the heart of the issue, and it struck wildly and strong. The young woman saw God's value for herself and the intention He had over her future marriage. She could picture what marriage was supposed to be, what God intended it to be, and it changed everything. It was part of what God had designed for her life, and she reset herself to the direction of true north inside.

Everything changed in a moment. She wasn't going to marry a man like her father; there was a good man for her, a man who would have a good nature, not an angry one. She also felt known by her friend praying for her because she had never told her about the verbal abuse, nor did she know how to articulate the pain of it filling her whole life from being around him.

I saw something different in this scenario than the one with the psychic medium. This wasn't just about viewing pieces of information in order to help bring some encouragement. This was God showing one of His intimately connected children information that could change the issues going on. It could also speak God's plan and intention over the future—one that could bring spiritual transformation or resolution in one minute to the entire veiny root system of corruption the girl had in her background or family line.

This young woman was transformed in a before-and-after moment that changed her forever.

DISCERNMENT

Discernment isn't just spiritual intuition, although intuition can be part of it. It's not just a feeling we get to know what is right or wrong or who is safe or unsafe, although that can be part of it as well. After I saw all that I did about the spiritual realm, the second heavens, I realized the full truth that God is at work—on layer upon layer of every part of the fabric of our lives—to restore us to what He dreamed. He is giving us access to know that work, and we *get to* partner with it through the spiritual gifts. Unattached from relationship with Him, though, spiritual gifts get distorted and don't bring change, transformation, resolution, or help. People see in the spirit outside of God leading them all the time, whether through a gift of how they were wired or by the enemy opening their eyes so that he can use and manipulate them.

Discernment is allowing us to see His intention over the spiritual realm by God's Spirit, and it is one of the most satisfying gifts we can have because we will feel completely in sync with this supernatural God we call Father.

Discernment is also one of the main catalysts to entering into the wisdom available to reign in life.

THE WOMAN CALLED WISDOM

"I want you to meet someone," the angel said as he took me back to the place before time began. We walked into an extraordinarily beautiful place that was so lush, so tropical, but so manicured. How could this much wildness and form fit so perfectly together! In the middle was a tree that had a stream coming out from beneath it. It was glorious. Then I looked beyond and realized we were on the top of a mountain, and I could see across to valleys of civilizations. It was like we were at the top of the world.

There at the stream, sitting at the base of the tree with her feet in the water, was a woman. She looked older than anyone I had ever seen, but instead of wrinkles telling me so, it was her eyes. They were ageless, but it was like everyone who ever lived wouldn't be as old as she was.

"Hello, Shawn," she said. When she said my name, I felt naked. I felt like I was fully known. I was aware of all that I wasn't yet and also aware of all of my flaws and even weaknesses. I am sure she was aware as well, but it didn't seem to be her focus. Then she smiled and patted the seat next to her and said, "Isn't it beautiful?" I sat down and put my feet next to hers in the water, and my whole being was filled with beauty, wonder, and powerful knowing.

It was like every problem there ever would be could be solved at the base of this tree. Every man who ever hated wouldn't hate anymore, if they could just look at this woman. Every court case could have a solution. Every world problem could have a resolution. The best way to describe it is that I could feel the *ultimate* truth, not just my truth or someone else's version of truth but God's will and nature of truth, over every issue I thought of. The best words to describe it were *full reality*. "I was before time; I was first," she said. Then I read Proverbs 8 with her out of the Bible, some of which I'll share here (but read it all on your own time—it's incredible).

> Can't you hear the voice of Wisdom? From the top of the mountains of influence she speaks into the gateways of the glorious city. At the place where pathways merge, at the entrance of every portal, there she stands, ready to impart understanding, shouting aloud to all who enter....For even the foolish and feeble can receive an understanding heart that will change their inner being. The meaning of my words will release within you revelation for you to reign in life....If you have an open mind, you will receive revelation-knowl-edge....I have at my disposal living-understanding to devise a plan for your life....You will find true success when you find me, for I have insight into wise plans that are designed just for you....For the fountain of life pours into you every time that you find me, and this is the secret of growing in the delight and the favor of the Lord.
> —PROVERBS 8:1–3, 5–6, 9, 12, 14, 35

She looked at me after we read it all and said, "I am the key to seeing God's heart. No one who is in pursuit of any spiritual matter will have relationship with me unless they are looking for His heart."

We sat for what seemed like an eternity, and she answered so many of my questions. So much of it went directly past my mind into my spirit, and the fruit of it was this: I became an everlasting optimist.

I know that Solomon was using poetry when describing the spiri-tual reality of wisdom, but God related it to me through an encounter so that you, with me, could see the value of seeing in the Spirit and how it is a process that's guided by the light of His wisdom. No other way will lead you to fulfillment or to the greatness of what the spiritual realm holds. *Without* her it is dangerous; *with* her it is an endless, glorious stream, flowing from the hidden fountains of His depths that lead you to the place of influence.

She gave me what looked like a rolled-up parchment and smiled as if she were giving me one of the most precious things she owned.

I opened it, and it was Proverbs 3:19–26.

Wisdom's Blueprints

The Lord laid the earth's foundations with wisdom's blueprints. By his living-understanding all the universe came into being. By his divine revelation he broke open the hidden fountains of the deep, bringing secret springs to the surface as the mist of the night dripped down from heaven.

Wisdom, Our Hiding Place

My child, never drift off course from these two goals for your life: to walk in wisdom and to discover your purpose. Don't ever forget how they empower you. For they strengthen you inside and out and inspire you to do what's right; you will be energized and refreshed by the healing they bring. They give you living hope to guide you, and not one of life's tests will cause you to stumble. You will sleep like a baby, safe and sound—your rest will be sweet and secure. You will not be subject to terror, for it will not terrify you. Nor will the disrespectful be able to push you aside, because God is your confidence in times of crisis, keeping your heart at rest in every situation.

As I looked at the document she gave me, I felt like it came from the deepest place of God. It contained secrets that were now being revealed. It was filled with blueprint revelation for lives: schematics for each of us individually.

"The connection to wisdom and to your purpose will help to define your character, your lifestyle, your family, your career, your happiness," she said. "When you lack it, it creates imbalance spiritually, mentally, emotionally. God is giving purpose and wisdom to humanity. It will be received in a way that has never been so in any generation, a way that will lead all the way to His return."

I thought about themes that are some of the most popular in our generation. Every stream of Christianity has books about developing the individual in their purpose and wisdom. It's really not just a phenomenon; it's an intentional plan of God.

Then the angel who had been with me came back and said, "We are going somewhere else," with a huge grin on his face. What could be better than what I was experiencing? Not just knowledge was flowing through me but also the intricacies of God's own musings about everything I asked. How could I leave this?

But the angel's look of excitement made me go.

CHAPTER 14

THE THIRD HEAVEN

SOMEONE I'M ACQUAINTED with, who is in union with Christ, was swept away fourteen years ago in an ecstatic experience. He was taken into the third heaven, but I'm not sure if he was in his body or out of his body—only God knows. And I know that this man (again, I'm not sure if he was still in his body or taken out of his body—God knows) was caught up in an ecstatic experience and brought into paradise, where he overheard many wondrous and inexpressible secrets that were so sacred that no mortal is permitted to repeat them. I'm ready to boast of such an experience, but for my own good I refuse to boast unless it concerns my weaknesses (2 Cor. 12:2–5).

∽

The angel grabbed my hand and took me up higher. When I got to where we were going, I knew exactly where we were—not because I am spiritual enough to understand or knowledgeable enough to relate, but it just was what it was. I was hovering in different places around the throne room of God and seeing His city. It seemed to come out from His being.

It was so awesome that it will not be easy to describe the many things I saw, but I want to frame a little of it.

Contrary to how most throne rooms are depicted in more modern times—with a throne at the head and people in various stances in front of the one who sits on it—this was far different. In the middle of the throne room was the Trinity. Somehow the One who does not fit in the time and space He created was there, enthroned. I saw the Father, who was too big to even fit; Jesus, the Man on the throne; and the Spirit hovering over them. They had a constant communication line going—a communion of thoughts, personhood, ideas, and enjoyment. It's indescribable. I was in awe.

Somewhere up above this empire, state-sized angels were shouting "Holy! Holy!" and I knew it was the cherubim, mentioned in Isaiah 6, who had been looking at God since they were created. They were measuring His glory, looking for His end, and in their whole creation, I don't think they had even made it in one full circle around God—that is how vast He was, yet somehow He fit. I cannot describe it. They were in awe, and I was in awe of their awe.

As I looked around, I saw four pillars that reached higher than I could see, positioned like points of a square around God. But these pillars had eyes and shapes, and they were alive and witnessing all that God was doing and helping the rest of heaven to connect to all God offered. They had the full perceptions of God over every micro detail, and they were alive like nothing I know has ever been. Their radiant joy in His majestic work, after watching it since time began, could not be described. They had enough eyes to see it all, and I knew that these were what John saw as the living creatures; I just did not know that they were so big. It seemed that if you put the four of them on top of each other, they would be the same measure of time itself. They were perfectly created to see all God was doing throughout our time and to keep a full record of His goodness and the response in man and all that would happen because of it.

Surrounding the throne, and on the outside of these incredible creatures, were twelve pillars of light that were like eternal beacons of His love. These were the twelve thrones of the apostles, the authority of His love that held the universe accountable to His truth. It came from those lights. I couldn't understand it, but I couldn't stop looking.

The ground underneath it all was like the largest ocean ever, but it was also like an augmented reality screen. I could see full projections of all God had ever done and all that He was doing all at once, but the artistry of how the images were put together was so visually stimulating that I felt like I was passing out whenever I looked at it. I wanted to watch the floor more than I have ever wanted to see any movie or watch any TV show on the earth. I could stare at it for thousands of years and never get enough of how His beauty has been interwoven in every story of mankind. All the mysteries of His love, justice, and creativity were there.

Then I was brought lower, and the angel had me land down on the ground of this place. That is when I realized just how vast it was. Was I an ant? But I did not feel insignificant. At the same time I didn't feel important compared to the beautiful, glorious, holy Trinity in front of me, who seemed to exude a joy that caused everything inside of me to spike. How could I ever go back to earth after this? Thank God I knew I was only seeing in part. It was as if the angel had turned the spiritual volume of what I could see down to a one out of infinity.

Then I looked across and could see so many more people—not just those who had graduated their earthly lives but who were here, like me, in visions and encounters.

One was an old man, but not any old man. I recognized him. I knew he was a man named Bob Jones on the earth. I had known about him from afar but had not met him yet. I could see he was here on assignment like me, not just experiencing the glory of this place. He was handing out orders to angels. No, really. He handed them rolled-up scrolls (that I am sure were parabolic, so I could understand what he was doing) and was telling them where to go.

"What kind of man gives orders to angels?" I whispered under my breath.

"Any kind of man who knows his authority," the angel next to me answered. This was unbelievable.

Then Bob saw me, and I saw him. We were both in a vision, yet this was real time. This wasn't just me in a spiritual imagination; these encounters were real, and we were seeing each other in heaven. We smiled a knowing smile at each other, and I knew we would know each other on earth. (As a side note, we met at the end of the next month, and the first words out of his mouth were, "I have seen you before, but where?" And when I told him it was in heaven, he announced to a group of us what he was doing and what I was doing and told the date of this encounter. We became fast friends all the way until his passing, and I learned a lot from him.)

This is the part in the story I detail in my book *The Throne Room Company*, which is about a people who are spending time with God the way we were all designed to: in connected communion to His heart through Christ. The Holy Spirit called these people "the throne room company" because they were more consumed with eternity than their natural lives or accomplishments. They were living their lives for Jesus to return but had incredibly fulfilling lives on the earth while doing it.

WHAT IS COMING

The angel took me higher than this again and said, "I am to show you what is coming."

I thought I was going to go into a vision like the one John wrote about in the Book of Revelation, but I did not. I saw what our eternity was like. I do not know if I can describe it, but I am homesick for it. It's beyond what we can hope for or imagine. As a matter of fact, when we imagine heaven, many of us just think about living in glorified mansions, flying around, eating all the food we want, and being friends with animals. These are not bad images, but they are not exactly the object of what our eternal existence is about.

Realize that God did not create anything to be destroyed. He never created man to fall. It was never His intention. Just as He gave us free choice, He immediately created an additional plan to His original plan that we could choose at any point and be restored. This restoration on this side of eternity looks like many things: restored families, rebuilt industries, discipled nations, churches that become the center of communities, ingenuity, and engineering—all from His original plans and thoughts. We are going to see a transformation that will bring Jesus the fullness of reward for the price He paid on the cross. We have a destiny of being a mature bride who knows how to walk with Him, partner with Him, and love Him the way He wants to be loved. But then what?

Hardly anyone talks about what eternity will be like. We have limited it to our picture of heaven, and it seems more like a Holodeck on the *Star Trek* show than an actual place that was God's original intention, reborn for us.

As a matter of fact, in the Book of Revelation John "saw 'a new heaven and a new earth.' For the first heaven and the first earth had passed away, and there was no more sea" (21:1, MEV). But the new heaven and earth he saw, which replaced the millennial heaven and earth, did not include the heaven where God dwells. The word *ouranos,* translated "heaven," used in this verse most likely refers to earth's atmosphere and/or space.[1]

John wrote that the first heaven and the first earth "pass away" (*parerchomai*), which some Bible scholars interpret to mean complete annihilation and others interpret to mean a renovation. Those who believe earth and heaven will one day no longer exist point to 2 Peter 3:7, which says "the heavens and the earth that now exist are being reserved for fire" (MEV). Those who believe the heavens and the earth will undergo a renovation relate it to the days of Noah, when the earth was covered by a great flood and a new kind of earth emerged when the waters receded.

The word translated "new" in Revelation 21:1 is *kainos*, and it means "a new kind" or "fresh."[2] Another Greek word for "new" is *neos*, meaning "young."[3] Because Revelation 21:1 says there will not be a sea on the new earth, we can be assured that this verse does not refer to the millennial earth, because large bodies of water will still exist during the millennium (Isa. 11:9; Ezek. 47:8–10, 15, 17–20; 48:28; Zech. 9:10; 14:8). Therefore, John must have been describing the eternal earth.[4]

THE NEW HEAVENS AND NEW EARTH

The second heavens are going to be renewed, and those tumors of demonic activity will be completely removed. The spiritual structure that was more like the cell system of eternity that God showed me will be fully restored to work the way it was supposed to.

The natural earth or the first heavens will also be restored, refreshed, renewed. God never intended anything He created to be destroyed.

Now, if you can follow this train of thought with me, what would everything look like if Adam and Eve hadn't fallen in the garden? Where would the earth be? What technologies would be expressed? What artistic expressions would be blanketing the earth? What cities and cultures would be built? What would man's relationship be to the animals of the earth, to the food systems of perennial plant life, to the universe that is ever expanding around us?

When you imagine eternity, do you picture yourself as a

superhero, flying around and enjoying your earthly retirement? Or do you understand that eternity, our everlasting God appointment, is actually going to pick up where Adam and Eve left off, only this time with a whole lot of redemptive stories that fuel our passion to create with God, to populate this universe He gave us and dwells in with us.

The first thing God did for Adam and Eve, as far as their role with Him, was to give them a job to steward creation. Adam began to name the animals, which was not just so he had something to call them. He was archiving them, discovering the value of each creature God made to the universe around him, seeing through God's eyes what the properties of their being were and how to take care of them and create with them, to understand their personalities, traits, and makeup. He would have been discovering horsepower and bees' pollination qualities. He would have been knowing, as he was building cities, which creatures were to help bear the burden, which ones were good for creating with man, and which ones were just part of the artistic ecosystem to be enjoyed.

God had planned how these animals and how this creation would be an ever-unfolding scenario around man and his stewardship of it, how this stewardship would be one of the greatest ways that humanity could constantly see an unfolding revelation of God's love, which only got deeper with each season of life spent in this place.

Is there life on other planets? If we had not gone off the rails of God's original plan, I am convinced we would already be space traveling and starting to uncover some of the greater mysteries of God in the universe around us, and possibly some of the ones next to us.

In our eternal scenario, we will be building in companionship to one another. That looks like nuclear families and people groups that form towns, cities, and regions and populate God's dream.

We will advance in science; in literature, which we will still be producing; in the arts, which we will always be leveling up; and in agriculture, which will be ever increasing in delightfulness, but the toil will be taken out. We will have recovered God's intention of work for the sake of relationship and satisfaction and knowing Him, not work for the sake of survival.

When you think of the coming age, is it really someplace you have thought you would have real estate in and a role to play, people to live with and grow with, God as your center, mysteries to explore, and places to experience? Or has it been more of a fairy-tale place that just feels more like magic than reality?

One of Our Greatest Divine Motivators Is Eternity

"One of the things the great maturing will bring will be a conscious hunger to be in eternity," the angel said, "not just to escape the world but because they'll have a vision of what is to come. People will stop living primarily for their earthly destiny when they see the value of their eternal one. Just as Jesus gave up the desire to be a natural Solomon—with a kingdom that could be fully understood in His one earthly lifetime—so people will give up their desires to fulfill every purpose that is in their hearts on this side of eternity and start to live with a divine hope that everything in them is going to be fully expressed there. They'll hope for a fulfillment that is beyond understanding when eternity is truly their home and destination. Their purpose on earth is like a shadow of what is there, pointing them at how good eternity will be!"

Anyone who is in a committed relationship likely cannot imagine their quality of life without that relationship. People who are in romantic love often say, "I wouldn't want to live or do life without you." People who are motivated by eternity understand this, and they can't wait to be face-to-face with Jesus in His fullness. Their eyes have seen it—they have seen the eternal life and are motivated by it even more than their motivation for a destiny, justice, or family on this side of eternity.

This also takes all pressure to be the "messiah" off of us on this side of eternity—when we know He has already come and is coming again to restart the whole universe and the spiritual realm and restore us to everything He dreamed.

CHAPTER 15

THE GREAT MATURING

I WAS IN SOUTH Korea ministering. I was poured out and ready to go back to the hotel. The pastor informed me that one of his elders was going to drive me and said he trusted him completely. I was escorted out to get into his car, and it was a very nice Mercedes sports car, a fun way to end the night. The man introduced himself as Daniel. I knew this was a spiritual moment; revelation hovered over us and gave us both a feeling of destiny.

As we were driving and making small talk, the man said, "I need to ask you something about your watch. Is it special to you?" It was a nice watch I had been given by someone in the ministry, along with a prophecy that a new season of breakthrough was coming into my life. It wasn't a luxury watch or anything extremely special to most people, but it had sentimental value because right after he gave it to me, we had a season of unprecedented ministry activity in our lives. The watch helped me to rest in each experience and opportunity and enjoy God in it.

Daniel said, "That makes what I am going to ask you difficult. I was wondering if you would exchange your watch for mine." I could not see his watch, but I felt like God was putting in his heart that he needed what my watch represented. I was willing, even without knowing him, because it felt right, even if it was a strange request.

I took off my watch and said, "You don't have to exchange; you can have this as a signpost."

But he said, "No, you don't understand; I need to give you my watch." He took his off and told me to put it on.

It was a luxury Swiss brand that had cost him a lot of money. "When I was in one of the hardest places financially, we were following God and it was very rough. Everything was leveraged in faith, and then the impossible happened. It was all paid off! I felt like God put it in my heart to buy that watch as a signpost of breakthrough, that the time had changed in my life. I want to sow that into your life—that this is a new time and that things that happen after this will mark your life as different from before."

I looked down at the watch and was buzzing. It was not just an expensive watch; it was also a prophetic word. The watch could build one whole school in a warzone through a nonprofit we are on the board of, but that was not what this was about. This was about God marking my time as different, and this is what he then said:

"I am Daniel, and I have a calling of Daniel of the Bible. You do too, and I feel like God is going to raise up partners who will bring about God's timing over projects, businesses, and God's efforts on the earth together. A lot of people are in desperate need of this because they have followed God, and it looks like the opposite is happening, but then you will show up as a Daniel and help them understand the time they live in and bring breakthrough."

As I put on the watch, I was stunned because I knew God was speaking.

The next night I was with a mainstream entertainment group that I regularly ministered to, and the Christian woman who runs the group asked me, "Where did you get that watch? It was God, wasn't it? Don't you remember my story?" And she told me her story again, but I had never known the brand of watch.

When she gave her business for South Korea to God, she signed an American actor to her agency to model and act. It seemed like a dying effort, and nothing was happening, but God had put it in her heart to bring him over. Then she was prophesied over that breakthrough was coming in her career and a contract would come. That next week, this watch's company hired her actor/ model. They paid him generously, like he was an A-list star, and as a gift to her he bought her one of these watches. Even though he was not a Christian, he believed in her faith and vision and was impacted by it, so he said, "Things will never be the same. Wear this to remember that." And they were not.

"We are twins," she told me. "What God is doing with you, He is doing in your industry, not just ministry." I knew from what she was saying that God was raising up the anointing on Daniels everywhere. I love that this happened to be a woman from South Korea—we can see there is no preference to God between man or woman or race.

Fast-forward a year.

The angel was again with me, and he made a huge statement: "In the great maturing, people will understand the times and seasons they are in and know what to do with their lives. Great resources and a great positioning will happen as people of faith get this revelation." He touched me, and I had a deep, revelatory encounter.

I saw people—like you reading this book—who have had encounters. Some of you even had an encounter, dream, or prophecy about being a Joseph, an Esther, a Daniel, a Solomon. I saw the Holy Spirit setting watches on your arms, setting your time to be new and significant. I saw God putting His Spirit that He called "overcomer" inside of you.

The First Year of Our Time in Los Angeles

During the first year of our time in Los Angeles, I had kidney stones seven times. They always hit on a Tuesday because Tuesday nights were when we did our ministry gathering. I knew they were demonic, but no matter how much I prayed, or others did, they kept coming, sometimes lasting for days. Remember the house I lived in? I slept in a room right above the gathering space for our meetings. I could hear the worship on these Tuesday nights, and I loved it. While I was in pain, I would cry out to God for everyone gathered and feel the pain and sufferings they had gone through; and I'd present them to God, asking for Him to make them champions and influencers, whole, full of love, in a family, and resourced.

On one particular night, I had my eyes closed as I prayed and rolled around in pain. I felt someone was standing next to me and thought, "Who on earth came into my room?" thinking maybe someone had violated a boundary. Then, when I looked up, I saw what looked like a biblical figure standing there. I heard an internal, audible voice saying, "Welcome the Deliverer!" I began to weep and realized I was totally healed. There were no more kidney stones after this, ever. I was so overwhelmed. I thought of all the people downstairs, and I knew so many had such real, present problems. I started to pray for their deliverance, and I was filled with the Father's heart and passion for them. I do not know that I have ever prayed like that.

But even so, I heard the voice say, "He has not come to just deliver them from all of that; He has come to deliver them *into* promise." And I heard in my spirit, "What would that look like?" I realized that I did not know. I was not thinking of each of them in the fullness of the Father's dream on this side of eternity, let alone all eternity. I was not imagining what their lives would look like if they were whole, full of His Spirit and power to take on their destiny purposes. I mean, of course I believed for them, but I didn't know what any of their promised lands would look like. Then I realized I didn't know what mine would look like.

"The promises of the overcomer are available in the Book of Revelation, not just to get away but to *occupy* the promise."

I knew God was contrasting it to the children of Israel, who had been in captivity for a long time, enslaved to the point where their Hebrew religion wasn't even easily accessible anymore. For four hundred years, the Israelites were crying out from their DNA, "Deliver us, God!" God promised them a land and a purpose, a restoration to all that He could do for them on this side of eternity—to prosper them, to dwell with them, to walk with them. I am sure their original mentality couldn't even fathom what a land of promise looked like. They were more in the mindset of "Can He really get us out of here?"

Moses did get them out, though, through the power of God's love for them. Not only were they about to go into a land and take possession of it; they also had all the best stuff of Egypt that the Egyptians had released to them. For forty years they carried around enough resources to create and craft and occupy a rich land and buy anything they wanted. They were still in a survival mindset, though, not an occupying mindset. They didn't know the flip side of their Deliverer. They didn't know what it was like to be given a land that flowed with every blessing they'd prayed for.

When they inherited it, God had to have them walk out spiritual, prophetic acts to claim the promises. They were confused by many things, and God had to answer their fears and care for their hearts as they went. The question as to why the land was already occupied is a prototype for us: the land was cultivated for hundreds of years before they even got there, so they did not have to build from scratch. When it was their time to occupy, they moved into houses furnished perfectly that they hadn't built, into cities elaborately designed that they hadn't architected. They were brought into one of the mysteries of what God does when He places His people into His purpose: He matches the resources to the maturity He has placed inside of them.

That night, when I had this encounter, I went down to my church healed and shared it with the whole group. I couldn't stop crying, but I said, "Let's ask God, who is our Deliverer, to give us a vision past our survival, past having to get out of hard things. Let's ask Him for a vision of what we look like in our promised land, what we are called to possess once there is wholeness and foundational health in our lives." God gave a lot of people in our small starter group visions that night that changed their lives.

He gave me a vision for you: when you cry out to see what your promised land is in this lifetime, then He will show you what life looks like past overcoming issues—if your aim is walking out your life for Him, really surrendered. He will show you what it looks like on this side of eternity and help you walk into part of what He dreamed before time began. You will be a promised land kind of person. People who run into you won't know what to do with the quality of life you live because of the relationship you have with God.

Wisdom is going to be a marking feature of the coming move of God.

Spiritual perspective is going to be your key to access the deeper life you want to walk out on this side of eternity. One of the largest spiritual wars on the earth right now is over perspective, the way you see possibilities or limitations; the way you see people groups, gender, and age; the way you are empowered by what God is doing or limited by what the enemy or man is doing wrong.

"People will substitute their spiritual connection with God for knowledge about spiritual and natural things," the angel told me one day. I didn't understand, but he took me back into the second heavens, and I saw the enemy's activity. As I watched them communicating, I realized these beings—that could only be in one place at one time and were puffed up in self-importance—really believed they were making a difference against God. When I looked for their power source, I could only find one: knowledge. I remembered that I had seen all of history and knowledge imprinted here. "They are like knowledge brokers," the angel said. "This is their only real power now—to know before anyone else and use that knowledge to destroy, connive, and threaten."

A knowledge broker is someone who extracts the knowledge and wisdom of experts, packages it into a mastermind deal, and sells it to the right audience. I saw these demonic entities act like twisted spiders, wrapping their lies and twisted perspectives around people. "Their best audience is unbelieving believers or people who have enough knowledge and connection to the religion of Christianity but no longer have, or never had, the heart for it," he said.

"Why is that their best audience?" I asked, not meaning to challenge. I'd thought people who had a trace of religion would be more mindful.

"Because they are people who have knowledge without faith, and they feel that spiritual or human growth, and maturing, is directly tied to how much and what they know," the angel said. "They have substituted knowledge for relationships. The enemy loves to feed them this narrative because he can get them focused on a cause, an issue of right and wrong, or a doctrine or philosophy and keep them trapped there, with no hope to change it in their lifetime."

It felt so wrong but was also so obvious. Keep people who would be some of God's best trapped in the prison of being experts on topics without having any hope of changing or resolving them.

I could see the demonic activity, the spider webs, and the collection of ideas being spread through social media and search engines into households faster than anything could be spread. Whether it was a political half-truth, a scientific offense, or a prophetic conspiracy, it spread like a fire into minds and then hearts, burning all the ground that had been prepared by God and keeping people in cycles of arrogant complacency. It was horrifying, and I found myself checking my own heart.

So many of these demonically inspired spiritual knowledge brokers were great arguers and awesome at shutting down a conversation but terrible about bringing any real sense of justice or moving forward.

Then I was brought into an awe-inspiring courtroom, with a judge in it who was perfectly fair—one with Solomon's wisdom or the Father's compassion. This judge was *only* going to be fair. This wasn't a time of just holding someone accountable for doing something wrong; this was a judge who was going to help settle important disputes—disputes that would cause perpetual disconnection and corruption (in areas God determined He would have victory in) if left unsettled.

I thought back on Solomon and how his wisdom cut through tons of arguments. His proverbs trained, and still train, people on how to reign at living with godly character. His truth went past mere knowledge, which can puff up, create arrogance, and disconnect us from the heart of a matter. He had God's perceptions, not just imparted knowledge. This was not a man giving philosophical truth; this was a revelatory man bringing spiritual resolution to important matters. When people walked away, justice had been served.

The one thing about the courtroom of heaven is that nothing is decided by knowledge, facts, or information alone. Decisions are measured against the heart of God and what God knows—which is often unseen and unknown, except for those who are looking for it. God presents options and resolutions that humans can't imagine, much like Jesus demonstrated opportunities, through His earthly life, that no one would have ever conceived of.

One of the distinguishers of this great maturing that is and will be taking place is that Christians will truly trust God. They will trust Him with their reputations and relationships, their need for heavenly justice and provision, and in their leadership roles. And they will trust His interests toward them.

Trust is so challenged in relationships today—toward media, toward government, toward education, toward local leaders, toward church leaders. God is not like man, though, and as this great maturing takes place, trust will be on display in Christianity. It will be a marker of maturity, and it's something you cannot fake or pretend.

CHAPTER 16

THE COMING MOVE OF GOD

WHEN I MET my wife to be, Cherie, she came to an event I was speaking at in Arizona with a few friends. I had them all come to the front, and I prayed destiny over each one of them. When I grabbed Cherie's hand last, she had a vision of us getting married outdoors under a tree. She had never met me before and knew from her spiritual training in ministry that this was not considered a good vision to have, but she could not deny it or its truth. She was imprinted by it.

Many years later, when I pursued her and after we were engaged, she told me about the encounter. I knew it was a profound one because God had opened my heart and drawn me to her so radically. We hired a wedding coordinator to help us arrange where to be married. We had a good-sized guest list, and we wanted to create an epic event since we had both waited so long to be married. We knew we were not just getting married for companionship, although she was already my best friend, but also for our appointed purpose from heaven. God had made us for each other, and we knew it with every part of our beings.

Cherie and the wedding coordinator could not find a spot, even after looking at close to seventy-five venues or more. It was almost comical. Then one became available that fit with our dates, and it was an outdoor venue, just like Cherie wanted. When she went to tour it, there was the tree from her vision, an eleven hundred-year-old oak tree. When she told me, all the prophetic words from Bob Jones and these encounters came back to me. I was consumed with the fact that God is calling us to be rooted, or be a righteous root system, in the land, but that it comes only when we take on the purposes and relationships He has for us.

I thought of those words in context to us getting married, and I knew God was showing me that He was bringing people into relationships of marriage and family but anointing them for divine purpose. This did not mean they had to do ministry or have a business together; it meant that their process of doing life, building their marriage, and creating the culture of family would be put on display and become a light to the world around them. The families God is raising up would be the salt of the earth in the next great move of God. Covenant marriages and healthy parenting would create the seedbed for God's seeds of the greatest harvest the world has ever known.

On our wedding day, when we stood under that tree, I was so present to the fact that God had created this moment for us and dreamed it from the beginning of time. He had stamped our day with prophetic significance. It was so profound to me. We rested in this truth.

We had our reception in an olive grove on the property, and I knew that too was prophetic. God was going to use marriages and families as the container and distributor of the oil of the next move of His presence. In other words, the anointing that can bring revival looks like family first. That is one of the reasons nuclear family is being so attacked and marginalized by the media and special interest groups—the enemy is trying to do a preemptive strike and put shame on people who come from a nuclear family.

WIRED FOR FAMILY

When I was with the angel of God, I was shown God's strategy over humanity, and I saw how we are also wired for family. We are wired for marriage, for parenting, for growing, for developing. We are wired for core relationships that only bring unique purpose when those relationships come. In fact, we are so wired for nuclear family and healthy relationships that when we stray too far from them, as a people group, it acts like a rubber band: the further we get, the more it stretches, and once it stretches to its limit, it will snap back into place. We are being stretched against family to a limit we never thought possible in our generation, but many who are at the furthest points of the stretch are about to snap back and help others come back into God's original intention over humanity.

The angel took me over two human minds. One was beautiful, full of pathways that lit up in the darkest night, like traffic in the biggest city in the world. It was so full of energy, expression, and connections. Then I looked at the other brain, and it had quadrants of deep thoughts and beautiful lights firing, but it wasn't illuminated like the first.

"What am I seeing?" I asked.

"One is a mind that is operating with the mind of Christ. It is a mind that is healthy and looks at boundaries God is setting as invitations to stay focused and directed into fulfillment. It looks at conviction of sin and a desire for holiness as tools that keep it living within the bounds of God's intention for health, life, and well-being.

"This other mind is the mind of someone who wants unlimited freedom, no boundaries, no direction. This is the mind of someone who wants their own way and marshals their own energy. It doesn't create the life they were intending, and rebellion breeds disconnection within."

Then we backed away from the minds, and I saw them overlapping our generation.

"God is releasing the greatest investment of His design—that He has ever made in a generation—to share His mind and His perceptions with humanity. He has matured this generation to be able to have a capacity to receive the strength of His thoughts and mind. This will be one of the most unique times in history. While this has been maturing, man's capacity for evil has also increased because the knowledge, when used wrongly, breeds all kinds of darkness. God is never going to keep what He intended away from His people just because some will misuse it."

It is amazing that God, even more than a good father on earth, is willing to give something to His children and then develop it while knowing that some will not serve Him with it. It's much like when Jesus spent time with the twelve disciples and invested into Judas just as much as the others, even though Judas would ultimately betray Him. He gave Judas the same opportunity to show us that He finds more value in releasing and entrusting His nature and purpose to us than in worrying about what evil we might do if we ultimately become self-serving.

God is even making our choices and options simpler and clearer, whereas sometimes popular psychology and herd mentality cause everything to be convoluted and confusing.

Then we looked up, and I saw a river coming from the throne of God. It was flowing down onto His people with His thoughts, His personhood, and His very nature and being, and we were beautiful yet had ever-increasing beauty, enough so that at some point Jesus won't be able to take it anymore and will jump off His throne to return to us!

THE GREAT MATURING IS GOING TO
LEAD TO GREAT TRANSFORMATION

THE ANGEL TOOK me again to the storehouse of heaven, but it looked different from when I had seen it before. Yes, the creative miracles were stored and ready, and there were new technologies of every type that could simplify every part of our lives, even in a way that we can't imagine today. There were property deeds to houses, buildings, studios, airplane hangars, Wall Street offices—every kind of thing you could imagine. There were vehicles that will be invented in our lifetime that make *The Jetsons* seem boring. There were energy sources and refinement processes that are going to be harnessed and discovered all over the earth. They will rival fossil fuels and current solar or wind energy. We will even find energies in space. Forms of entertainment are going to emerge that will create entire industries from just sports, movies, Broadway shows, TV, and video games, and I also saw the resources to impact the forms of entertainment that already exist. There are educational plans, curricula, and creativity in the storehouse of heaven for the whole world to advance with, and shared spaces between nations for kids to learn from each other.

There is so much there that God has stored, and particular resources were tagged for us, before time began, for the works He predestined us for. It is abundant!

Then we went to another part of the storehouse, where I saw more things that had been prepared from the Father's heart. In this place were huge containers filled with groups of people. On the outside was a door with what looked like a timer on it. When the timer was set to go off, I saw that they would emerge, glowing with the brilliance of the mind of Christ. I could see the inside of their spirits, and it looked like an entire universe was in there. They held the power of God's very thoughts.

"This is the incubation happening that God had planned. He is using believers to help create safe places for His mind, will, and perceptions to be received on the earth."

"This is awesome, but what does this do?" I asked, because it seemed so mystical to be looking at a type of universe being born inside of people. I have no better language for this. It was majestic and supernatural, and it was happening to groups of people at a time.

Then he pointed at one of the different groups.

"They are a humanitarian organization looking at the educational system in a country in Africa. They aren't just looking at basic education; they are dreaming dreams with the Father and perceiving His original design over Africa and the people who live on the continent. They are seeing education's role in bringing transformation to systems of government, military systems, judicial systems, police forces, agriculture, and more. They are realizing a method of educating children that will prepare the children to be leaders in their nation in about thirty years' time. They have a mastermind connection going with each other, but it's being inspired by the brilliance God put inside of them to not just affect a school, a city, a region, or a nation; they are dreaming of what a developed Africa could look like, and they are going to use the tool of transformed education to develop that dream."

Then he pointed to another group in incubation.

I saw a financial company, or a group of people, working together on investment groups and a new form of banking that was so outside the box I couldn't understand it. I somehow knew I wasn't just seeing potential as the brilliant strategies filled them; I knew it was going to work. They were creating fair, equitable trading that could help the masses with much less risk and much more shared reward. What was this?

Then I saw a group within the group that was creating what I could only describe as an anointed hedge fund that would fund some of the greatest businesses driven by God's purpose. The group behind it seemed to consist of several families who were banding together to create greater impact that could actually bring transformation. They were just about incubated, and it was awesome.

There were so many more incubators growing God's ideas to maturity—over social justice issues, over people groups, over industries, over psychology and science and education. Can you imagine walking into a group of people who are discussing one of your passion interest areas? Imagine they are speaking with brilliant thoughts about intelligent ways to articulate problems and possible solutions. Imagine they are commissioned with God's very thoughts and strategies and are deployed to change the status quo on the earth.

I was awestruck. I knew that when people were impacted by these incubated dreams of God on the earth, they would be like Hiram or Sheba were to Solomon (1 Kings 5 and 10) and realize the love of God. They will be changed by the brilliance of God and say, "Surely God loves the world because He raised up a person like you!"

A lot of our future salvation in the days to come will be out of glorious moments like these. People will see what believers are accessing and will know God is not only real, but that He loves them too.

The storehouse of heaven is incubating maturity right now in believers all over the earth. Some of them are ready, or almost ready, and will be deployed in our lifetime to bring changes, solutions, inventions, creativity, and justice that will put on display the central theme of everything: for God so loved the world...

THE LAST ENCOUNTER

In the final part of this series of encounters, I could see, in the distance of time, the impending return of Jesus. I was so excited! We are not so far off now. It is not so far away. I have no idea if it will happen in my lifetime or my grandkids', but it is not fifty more generations away. He is coming, and He is maturing and developing a people who can't wait to meet Him—

- a people who have eternity on their hearts and love to dream with Him,

- a people who can't wait for His original plan and intention to come about to be in their fullness, and

- a people whose promised land is not found in the purpose they get to complete on this side of eternity but who get to do this while burning to be with Him where He is forever.

God has created us from before time began to share His nature and to work with Him. He has sent His Son, Jesus, to restore all things, and Jesus gave us the keys to do it. Through these encounters, you have a new perspective on how God is seeding Christians with everything we need to bring transformation to the world around us. Hopefully your faith and imagination have grown for what is available, and you have greater understanding on how God wants to root you into the ground of your purpose—the one He created you for from before time.

Most importantly, God wants to share His perceptions, wisdom, and inner process with you. He has given us the Bible and His Spirit to do this, and our generation is quickly going to see one of the greatest outpourings of transformation in the world, greater than any generation has ever seen. We are going to have an understanding of spiritual things that will become common thought, insights that only the wisest spiritual thinkers had before. God is distributing spiritual intelligence and advancing the world, and things are accelerating at a pace never seen before. It will become greater and greater as we get closer and closer to the return of Jesus.

I pray that the eyes of your understanding would be opened now as you finish reading this book so you too can experience everything you need to and that the great maturing I saw over and over through these encounters would happen to you!

ABOUT THE AUTHOR

S HAWN BOLZ IS a TV host, an author, a producer, and a Christian minister. He has been leading conversations in the church, entertainment industry, and in social justice that have helped believers connect their faith to culture in a transformative way.

Shawn's deeply connected yet humorous style of speaking, media hosting, and coaching through his unique expert perspective has brought him around the world to meet with churches, CEOs, entertainers, and world leaders. His voice is sought after in media, television, and podcasts where you can regularly find him being interviewed. His areas of passion include developing Christianity that brings transformation, the intersection of Christianity and popular culture, business from a faith perspective, social justice through faith, and hearing God's voice with a focus on restoring dignity to biblical, prophetic ministry.

He is the author of several best-selling books, including *Translating God*, *Keys to Heaven's Economy*, *Breakthrough: Prophecies, Prayers and Declarations*, and *Through the Eyes of Love*, and coauthor of *Wired to Hear*. Shawn is also a contributing journalist online to CBN News Network and Charisma News Network.

Shawn currently hosts *The Exploring Series*, which includes *Exploring the Prophetic* and *Exploring the Marketplace* podcasts, on Charisma Podcast Network, as well as *Discovering God* on TBN. You can also watch his YouTube series, *Your Prophetic Journey*, at the @bolzministries YouTube channel.

Shawn lives in Los Angeles with his wife, Cherie, and their two daughters, two dogs, cat, and five chickens.

NOTES

Chapter 1

1. For more on the revelation of the word *šāma'*, see Shawn Bolz, *God Secrets* (Studio City, CA: ICreate Productions, 2017).

Chapter 2

1. Blue Letter Bible, s.v. "*sōzō*," accessed August 5, 2021, https://www.blueletterbible.org/lexicon/g4982/kjv/tr/0-1/.
2. Blue Letter Bible, s.v. "*dynamis*," accessed August 5, 2021, https://www.blueletterbible.org/lexicon/g1411/kjv/tr/0-1/

Chapter 3

1. Frank Graff, "The Mighty Oak," UNC-TV, accessed August 6, 2021, http://science.unctv.org/content/mighty-oak.
2. "Oak Becomes America's National Tree," Arbor Day Foundation, December 10, 2004, https://www.arborday.org/media/pressreleases/pressrelease.cfm?id=95#:~:text=15%2C%202004%2D%2DAmerica%20has,designating%20the%20oak%20in%20November.
3. "The Symbolic Meaning of Oak Trees," Katy Tree Farm (blog), October 6, 2017, http://www.katytree.farm/blog/symbolic-meaning-oak-trees/.

Chapter 6

1. Jacob Hoschander, *The Book of Esther in the Light of History* (Philadelphia, PA: Dropsie College for Hebrew and Cognate Learning, 1923).

Chapter 7

1. "Christians Hold Largest Percentage of Global Wealth: Report," *Economic Times*, January 14, 2015, https://economictimes.indiatimes.com/news/company/corporate-trends/christians-hold-largest-percentage-of-global-wealth-report/articleshow/45886471.cms?from=mdr.

Chapter 11

1. Bob Jones and Bobby Conner, "Bob Jones and Bobby Conner: Dread Champions: Stand Up and Arise!," Elijah List, November 5, 2010, http://www.elijahlist.com/words/display_word/9295.

2. "Research Shows That Spiritual Maturity Process Should Start at a Young Age," Barna Group, November 17, 2003, https://www.barna.com/research/research-shows-that-spiritual-maturity-process-should-start-at-a-young-age/; "Evangelism Is Most Effective Among Kids," Barna Group, October 11, 2004, https://www.barna.com/research/evangelism-is-most-effective-among-kids/.

Chapter 14

1. Blue Letter Bible, s.v. "*ouranos*," accessed August 13, 2021, https://www.blueletterbible.org/lexicon/g3772/kjv/tr/0-1/.
2. Blue Letter Bible, s.v. "*kainos*," accessed August 13, 2021, https://www.blueletterbible.org/lexicon/g2537/kjv/tr/0-1/.
3. Blue Letter Bible, s.v. "*neos*," accessed August 13, 2021, https://www.blueletterbible.org/lexicon/g3501/kjv/tr/0-1/.
4. "What Does Revelation 21:1 Mean?" Got Questions Ministries, accessed August 13, 2021, https://www.bibleref.com/Revelation/21/Revelation-21-1.html.